Pensacola: Florida's First Place City *is sponsored by the Pensacola Historical Society as part of its continuing service to the community for historical research and museum interpretation and publication of Pensacola history. With generous gifts, Gulf Power, AmSouth Bank of Florida, and Gannett Foundation made publication of this book a reality. Society officers and members express their gratitude to the underwriting institutions and to all others—members, historians, friends of the Society—who generously shared research, knowledge, and encouragement for preparation of this narrative of Pensacola history richly illustrated with rare photos from the Society's collection.*

Mrs. Mayhew Wilson (Peggy) Dodson, President June Blome, First Vice President; William G. Champlin, Second Vice President; Garnier B. Minnich, Secretary; Mary Veal, Treasurer; Marjorie Hart, Parliamentarian; Virginia Parks, Historian; past president, Lou Ray; board of directors, W. D. Bach, G. Edison Holland Jr., Pam Shelden, Laura Keene, Martin Lewis, Theo D. Baars Jr., Vicent J. Margiotti, H. O. Anson Jr., Betty Gilmore, John E. Hodges Jr., Harry D. Kahn, and Laurence C. Scott; and curator Sandra L. Johnson

THE
DONNING COMPANY
PUBLISHERS
NORFOLK/VIRGINIA BEACH

PENSACOLA

FLORIDA'S FIRST PLACE CITY

A PICTORIAL HISTORY

JESSE EARLE BOWDEN · GORDON NORMAN SIMONS · SANDRA L. JOHNSON

GORDON NORMAN SIMONS

1937-1989

Authors Jesse Earle Bowden and Sandra L. Johnson
dedicate this book to the memory of Gordon Norman
Simons, archaeologist, historian, museum curator,
colleague, and friend, who inspired the conception of
this book and whose premature death prevented him
from seeing it to its final completion.

The Donning Company/Publishers,
5659 Virginia Beach Boulevard,
Norfolk, Virginia 23502

Edited by Holly Boden Nuechterlein
Richard A. Horwege, Senior Editor

Library of Congress Cataloging-in-Publication Data:
Bowden, Jesse Earle, 1928-
   Pensacola: Florida's first place city: a pictorial history /
narrative by Jesse Earle Bowden; compilation of
photographs and captions by Norman Simons and Sandra
Johnson.
   p.   cm.
   Bibliography: p.
   Includes index.
   ISBN 0-89865-777-6
   1. Pensacola (Fla.)—History—Pictorial works. 2.
Pensacola (Fla.)—Description—Views. I. Simons,
Norman. II. Johnson, Sandra (Sandra L.) III. Title.
F319.P4B68 1989   89-11871
975.9′99—dc20   CIP

Printed in the United States of America

Acknowledgments

The authors and the Pensacola Historical
Society express appreciation to many
Pensacolians who generously provided guidance
and assistance and shared information for this
book, especially Society Historian Virginia Parks,
who read early drafts; Pensacola writer/historian
Mary Dawkins, who prepared the index; Museum
assistant curator Sandra Ridley and volunteer
Len Leonard, who helped with picture
preparation. Special photographs were provided
through the generosity of Dean DeBolt of the
University of West Florida, Cooper Yates of
Hemmer & Yates Advertising Agents, and Al
Alderman of ASA Photo/Graphics. And we
express enduring gratitude to Florida and
Pensacola historians and writers whose
publications are in the selected bibliography and
to the many photographers through the years.
They made research and picture selection a
pleasant and rewarding task.

The arches at Fort Pickens lead us back in time to seek adventures of its past.
Richard Freeman

The Spanish flavor details the new Christ Episcopal Church at Wright and Palafox streets.
Constance H. Marse

Contents

Pensacola's modern 1989 skyline gives little hint of its long past, but nestled in among the glass and concrete structures are the brick and wooden buildings and preserved streetscape from the past 180 years.
Al Alderman, ASA Photo/Graphics

Prologue

Many Are the Flags

Striking the spit of sand the Spanish call the Isle de Santa Rosa and a sister barrier the Americans name Perdido, the northern blue waters of the Gulf of Mexico touch the tranquil, spacious harbor of Puerto de Ochuse.

For the first Europeans, turning eyes north from the Caribbean, probing mysteries of New World wilderness, it's the *best*—best bay; best port in the Indies.

Still, two sugary duned barriers embrace La Florida's westernmost seagates, hugging the harbor coast in nature's ever-changing yet enduring symmetry. Tides mirror the gold of the sun and the silver of the moon, zigzagging starlets of light across the wide yawning harbor of many names.

Swept by the centuries and the shifting sands of history, the harbor lures countless conquistadores, seafarers, explorers, soldiers, immigrants, dreamers, city builders.

Unseen, lingering in muted timelessness, ghosts of three centuries of colonial discovery echo the western epoch of La Florida history—tortured beachhead for origins of Spanish North America.

But long before the first Spaniards, wandering aborigines share the harbor, their traces of culture along the rivers and streams from the Apalachicola Valley and Choctawhatchee Bay to the Perdido River and Mobile Bay dating back ten thousand years. By the sixteenth century, Europeans stepping ashore call their descendant tribes fishing the harbor waters Apalachee, Choctaw, Chickasaw, Creek, Mobile, *Panzacola.*

Rising around the bay, ribboned by verdant live oak and pine pencilled against the horizon, shadowed by the U.S. Navy's Epic of Flight, La Florida's westernmost city basks in its fifth century claiming five flags—Spanish, French, British, Stars and Stripes of the 1821 Americanization of Andrew Jackson, and briefly, proudly, destructively, Stars and Bars of the Confederate States of America.

Yet the harbor is ever destined to become American, shadowed by its American conqueror Andy Jackson, who storms the Spanish town twice as soldier; then returns in peaceful flag exchange as first governor.

Still the mood of the harbor and time-weathered landmarks bespeak European and English origins.

Seabirds, winging and wheeling over the seagates, squawk shrill chants as they doubtless did early in the sixteenth century when Spanish captains first came, their sun-gilded sails casting a network of shadows on unknown waters of the bay the Indians called Panzacola.

Their toehold on the New World is often erased by turmoil and tides of nature and history.

7

The U.S. Naval Aviation Museum established in 1975 has emerged as a national shrine, attracting thousands of visitors annually.
U.S. Navy photo

Baylen Street Slip has new life in 1989.
Al Alderman, ASA Photo/Graphics

Still, seafarers, captains of colonization, and padres enter the harbor with dreams of gold and glory and settlement, carrying the flag of Spain, with musket, Christian cross, sword and cannon; desirous of Christianizing the savage and staking claims for king and country.

The harbor is a touchstone of a New World north of the Caribbean, envisioned by lusting conquistadores as a dusky, voluptuous goddess robed in the riches of magnificent discovery; a port of entry on the Gulf of New Spain with lands beyond the bay ripe with the promise of an earthly paradise scarcely less fruitful than Eden itself.

Here, with mists of saltspray, ancient brick and mortar, silent armament and remnants of the old Navy Yard that began when Pensacola was but four years American, La Florida adventurers bring many *firsts* to the discovery and development of the North American continent.

Among them, *Panzacola,* or *Pensacola.*

It begins as a navigator's mappoint; it becomes a City of History—a gumbo of cultural and ethnic heritage.

Pensacola chronicles its own long list of historical firsts—a perception inspiring proud Pensacolians through the city-building years of the twentieth century to challenge the Ancient City, St. Augustine, over *first* rights to historical longevity and for a share in the origins of La Florida.

For native Americans fishing its shores it's Sweet Water Country; for a polygot of entrepreneurs and immigrants bridging the nineteenth and twentieth centuries it's the ambitious Deep Water City; for airmen early in the twentieth century it's the Cradle of Naval Aviation and the Annapolis of the Air.

Naturally, the bay is first.

First for Spaniards, seeking a competitive edge over ambitious Frenchmen and Englishmen settling the New World; for Spanish hero Bernardo

de Galvez, defeating the British in the largest military siege on the Gulf Coast and removing the Union Jack from Southern waters during the American War for Independence; for Jacksonian Americans, carving the first two territorial countries from the old Spanish West and East Florida provinces; for territorial legislators beginning Florida's lawmaking legacy at Gull Point on Escambia Bay; for Southern secessionists, guarding a vital port in the American holocaust searing and dividing a young nation in civil war; for American lumber barons and timbercutters harvesting the ubiquitous pine and hardwood for world markets; for deep-water fishermen netting red snapper for domestic markets; for U.S. Navy air warriors pioneering flying machines and launching their evolution of a special adventuring breed who wear wings of gold.

By the New Pensacola Renaissance of the last three decades of the twentieth century—the preserved Old City, revitalized bayfront, changed skyline and streetscape—Pensacolians sloganize their harbor town as *Florida's First Place City*.

And many roots of Spanish La Florida— spreading uncharted wilderness claims across all of the present-day southeastern United States— grow from the discovery of the empire's westernmost harbor. Pensacola shares La Florida's beginning on the shores and the red cliffs of the virtually land-locked bay Spanish nobleman Tristan de Luna's sailors call "the best port in the Indies."

Shimmering sea and gleaming white sand of Pensacola Beach, circa 1989. Al Alderman, ASA Photo/Graphics

Aerial of Fort Pickens now preserved as a part of Gulf Islands National Seashore, circa 1989. Al Alderman, ASA Photo/Graphics

This 1562 Diego Gutierrez map labels explored areas such as Coosa, Apalache, and River Santa Elena, and River de Espirito Santo.
Library of Congress

1

Spanish Eyes North

The long peninsula Juan Ponce de Leon calls La Florida—carved into the nation's longest coastline by fate of the Earth's power—is irrevocably part of the Caribbean.

So too is the geographic fate of Spanish colonizers, awakening from medieval culture with dreams of conquest in the New World of Adm. Christopher Columbus. They find gold, silver, and glory in Peru and Mexico, carving out empires in Central and South America.

Their eyes turn north.

And their journeys lead them to Puerto de Anchusi or Santa Maria de Ochuse, names changing with the centuries and the flags until it becomes Pensacola Bay.

None can know the first European whose eyes see the bay following fabled East and West Coast discoveries of Ponce de Leon, *adelantado* of Bimini. Still, it is here, into what becomes *Bahia de Panzacola,* that Spaniards see and enter in the exploratory years after the fated Easter of 1513 when Ponce de Leon had found the magic land of flowers on the Atlantic coast on a bright April day, just twenty-one years after Columbus opened the New World, and named the peninsula for *Pascua Florida*—Feast of Flowers.

In 1519, Alonso Alvarez de Pineda, skirting the northern coast to the Mississippi River, may have seen the bay as he records the coastline for the first representative map of the Gulf Coast.

Adventuring Spaniards probe elsewhere in bays, harbors, inlets, and coves, yet it is Puerto de Anchusi—charted by Capt. Francisco de Maldonado in 1538—that Viceroy Luis de Velasco of New Spain selects for occupying and colonizing legendary lands of America envisioned by Ponce de Leon, Panfilo de Narvaez, and Hernando de Soto.

And blazing trails doomed to failure, the Narvaez and Soto expeditions bring the best harbor on the Gulf into the dreams of equally intrepid explorers.

Among the first, is the tall, red-bearded, one-eyed Panfilo de Narvaez, the image of a brave and resourceful soldier. He has twenty-six years of royal service in the New World when King Charles I awards him settlement rights of all La Florida.

Landing at Tampa Bay with four hundred men in 1528, Narvaez and his chief executive, Alvar Nunez Cabeza de Vaca, search for the mystic northern land Apalachee, near the present site of Tallahassee. But, marching inland, they lose contact with the fleet, which turns back toward Cuba. They soon discover they cannot feed themselves; aboriginal bowmen, swamps, and other miseries of the hostile land scatter and swallow the expedition. Survivors kill their horses for food, construct five rough-hewn wooden

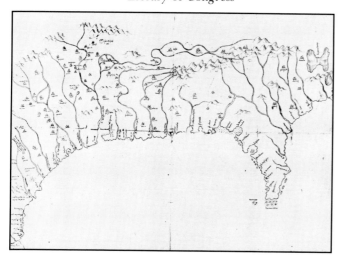

Circa 1544 anonymous map drawn during the Soto Expedition's search for gold throughout most of the American southeast.
Library of Congress

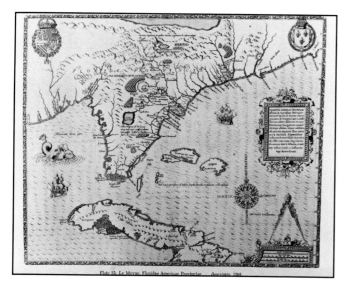

This 1591 map of Florida is by the Frenchman Le Moyne, well-known for his detailed drawings of the Timuca Indians of northeast and central Florida.
Published by De Bry

boats—fifty men to the vessel—and float westward along the Gulf Coast into uncertainty. Some wandering survivors clash with Indians at Pensacola Bay. Floundering in the surf westward to Matagorda, many drown or perish, including Narvaez; eighty survivors are cast up on the Texas coast.

Eight years later Cabeza de Vaca and three other survivors appear in Mexico, having walked thousands of miles. Vaca writes an epic narrative, verifying discovery of the bay—a grave for his countrymen.

Undaunted by Narvaez's misfortune, Don Hernando de Soto, at thirty-eight, expands the footprints of others. Desperate tales chronicled by Cabeza de Vaca merely spur him to "conquer, pacify and populate" the peninsula and lands westward to the Rio Grande.

King Charles gives Soto—wealthy from his Peruvian plunder—the Florida lands in the mid-1530s. Inheritor of the spirit of Columbus, the gold-seeking Spaniard sails into Tampa waters in 1539 with six hundred men in ten ships, naming the bay Espiritu Santo—Holy Spirit.

Lured north into the unexplored expanse by the dream and tales of wealth, Soto winters at Apalachee. His captain, Francisco de Maldonado, leads a reconnaissance into Pensacola Bay seeking a rendezvous harbor for the Soto expedition; he's impressed with its spaciousness. Soto sends Maldonado to Cuba for provisions, assuring his officer he'll return to the coast late in 1540.

Marching north on his indomitable procession, Soto moves through central and northern Georgia, circles through the westernmost portions of the Carolinas, and traverses parts of Alabama, Tennessee, Louisiana, and possibly Texas. He discovers and describes rich Alabama-Georgia-Tennessee lands he calls Coosa, lush for agriculture and for settlement.

For the next two years, Captain Maldonado returns to Pensacola Bay, awaiting Soto. He never arrives.

Drawn into his wide, sweeping march by Indian assurances of gold in the interior, Soto moves north and west but finds only the golden waters of the Mississippi River, which he names *Rio Grande de La Florida;* and there he dies, his corpse cased in a hollowed cottonwood log and slipped secretly into the waters he'd discovered to avoid desecration by Indians who believed him immortal.

Again survivors—sick, starving, fevered—make it back to New Spain. They condemn La

Florida as a land of bogs and poisonous fruits, barren, the very worst country warmed by the sun.

The dense American wilderness closes behind the Soto expedition, breathing again primeval air. Yet the harbor of Captain Maldonado awaits others.

Spaniards value two bays that grow in their dreams of settling La Florida in their New World race with the French and English. On the Gulf, Ochuse is considered the best, even though the Spanish are confused as to the difference between the bays that became Mobile and Pensacola.

The other, Puerto de Santa Elena, on the South Carolina coast and Port Royal Sound (Parris Island), is considered strategically more important, based on the eastern seaboard findings by Lucas Vazquez de Ayllon, who perished in a failed attempt to colonize San Miguel de Gualdape on the Atlantic in 1526. With this failure Spanish attention turns toward the Gulf entrance to the hinterland.

Together, the Maldonado-Soto-Ayllon findings ultimately focus on Ochuse for the first settlement leading to other colonies across the southeast with the major base at Santa Elena.

The challenge falls to Don Tristan de Luna y Arellano.

Born wealthy, son of the noble family of Borobia in Castille, Tristan de Luna seeks New World glory as a young adventurer in 1530 when he joins his cousin Antonio de Mendoza, first viceroy of New Spain. Ten years later he's marching as a cavalier and Maestro de Campo (chief of staff) with Francisco Vasquez de Coronado in his Southwest expedition, searching for the Seven Cities of Cibola. With nearly thirty years of loyal service in the New World, Don Tristan emerges as a brave, skillful captain who quells a major Indian uprising in Osxaca.

Marrying a wealthy widow, Luna seals his reputation as a hardworking and religious leader, loyal to the Crown, with assets to help finance another colonization venture. He is ideally suited to Viceroy Luis de Velasco's assignment as governor and captain general of La Florida and Santa Elena on November 1, 1558. At a ceremony in Mexico City, Governor Luna's expectations soar: he vows to bring Florida under Spanish banner, settle the land and protect its inhabitants for the king of Spain.

With five hundred recruited soldiers and more than one thousand others—women, children,

Don Carlos de Siquenza y Gongora, circa 1700, chief mapmaker of Spain and professor of mathematics at the Royal University of Mexico.
Pensacola Historical Society

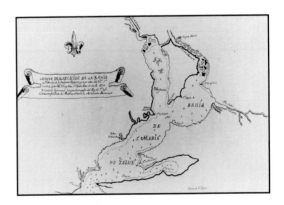

This 1693 map by Siquenza is the first known survey of the bay. It includes depth soundings and features, discovered by the Pez Expedition, such as Robledad (Grove of Oaks) and Baratillo (Junk Shop) site of Indian encampments where buffalo had been cooked.
Pensacola Historical Society

artisans, blacks and one hundred Aztecs — Luna sails in thirteen vessels. But his ordeal is stormy: He faces a revolt of his command before leaving Mexico City and the Yucatan; he's blown off course, and out of the confusion during the two-month voyage, he first enters Mobile Bay. Realizing Ochuse is eastward, he orders the surviving horses driven overland while the fleet searches for the harbor. On the eve of the feast of the Assumption of the Blessed Virgin Mary, August 14, 1559, he enters the bay. He writes King Philip II: "I set sail on June 11, and until the day of our Lady of August, when it pleased God that the entire fleet should enter the port of Ochuse. As we entered on the day I say, I named the bay in your honor as Bahia Filipina del Puerto de Santa Maria."

The Spanish nobleman reports, "Seamen say it is the best port in the Indies." He sees a "high point of land which slopes down to the bay where the ships come to anchor." He learns no secret, and writes, "It is somewhat sandy . . . I judge that it will not yield much bread." But he, like others since, sees forests of pine and live oak—a wooded wilderness ripe for harvest.

Luna's settlers are ready for their planned settlement—monastery, church, governmental buildings, houses, all enclosed by a stout wall. Unloading only half of their supplies on the beach, the Spaniards are in no hurry; they spend days playing in the water; racing horses and boats.

But trouble brews.

A hurricane destroys seven to ten ships, leaving Luna only a bark and a caravel; ruins food supplies and claims most of the livestock. The few local aborigines are no comfort; they refuse to provide food, labor, or information about the region.

Desperate, Luna seeks help from New Spain for his destitute and starving colony, then dispatches a food-seeking expedition into the wilderness to locate the aboriginal village of Nanipacana, mentioned in the Soto narratives. But the aboriginals, living in small settlements in the Alabama River country, flee, leaving behind supplies of corn and beans. Despite momentary relief, Luna is hesitant to relocate to Nanipa-cana, fearing he'd miss the promised relief ships.

Quarrels develop among the beleaguered soldiers and settlers; and Luna, ill and irritable, sees his grand plan collapse in misfortune and inefficiency. Tensions increase as the ill-tempered Luna orders forays along the Alabama River and

Coosa country. Moving his small army to Coosa, Luna finds the aboriginal supplies exhausted; his trusted advisers rebel.

Again the dwindling colony relocates on Ochuse bay, but both military leaders and Dominician friars mutiny against Luna's instability and stubborn unwillingness to abandon the settlement. Ordered to Santa Elena to guard against the French and Scots, Luna dispatches two frigates and a small bark to the Atlantic Coast, but a storm forces the crippled vessels back to New Spain.

Finally, soured by news of Luna's behavior, the angered viceroy in New Spain sends a new commander, Angel de Villafane.

Arriving in the spring of 1561, Villafane tactfully dismisses Luna and authorizes his return to Spain by Havana. Even for Villafane, the settlement is hopeless. By the summer of 1561, he evacuates the surviving two hundred colonists to Cuba in three ships and organizes the remaining contingent for an expedition to Santa Elena. But he too meets the fate of Luna. Arriving at Santa Elena June 14, a tropical storm inflicts such damage on his seventy-five man force he returns to New Spain defeated.

Luna, stripped of his governorship in disgrace, seeking reimbursements for portions of his personal fortune depleted in his aborted mission, tries to convince royal officials that subordinates wronged him.

But his petition is denied; Luna goes into oblivion, scorned by the Crown with whispers he failed to settle Florida. His only comfort, if any, is being among the first La Florida governors and surviving the wilderness ordeal, even if the beginning of the written history of Pensacola is stained by memories of disloyal lieutenants and wickedness of nature. Only hounding creditors break his solitude until his death.

By September 1561, frustrations of the Luna-Villafane failure doubtless prompt Philip II to announce Spain is finished trying to colonize inhospitable La Florida.

Yet the often deliberating, procrastinating Spanish fear others sailing Atlantic and Gulf coasts. And Philip II, motivated by fears of French encroachment in the Carolinas, changes his mind. In 1562, French Huguenots, led by Jean Ribault, land in Florida but the colonizers fail. Two years later the French land at the St. Johns River and build Fort Caroline.

With armed French threatening Spanish sea lanes, Philip dispatches Adm. Pedro Mendendez de Avilas to rid Florida of French transgressors. On August 28, 1565, the feast day of St. Augustine, Mendendez reaches Cape Canaveral and sails north seeking the French. He finds Ribault's fleet at the St. Johns but the French vessels flee. He turns southward to a harbor he names San Agustin de La Florida (St. Augustine).

Mendendez, armed with all the continental intelligence of his less-fortunate predecessors, and with strategies encompassing territories from Newfoundland to the east Gulf Coast, aims for settlements on fertile lands near Santa Elena. He envisions a fortified settlement at Coosa, thus fulfilling Viceroy Velasco's plan of empire so painfully shattered by the failing Luna expeditions. Despite hardships and French attacks that led to the slaughter of the French at the bloody Matanzas massacre, St. Augustine survives—now the oldest continuously occupied settlement in the United States.

Slowly, nudged by the sweep of New World colonization, the Spanish await destiny, however fragile their foothold, however uncertain La Florida possessions. With settlement of St. Augustine, Spanish padres build missions into Apalachee to the Gulf at St. Marks.

And Bahia Santa Maria Filipino de Ochuse remains little more than a sandpit on Spanish maps, remembered for the Luna expedition failure and neglected more than 125 years.

The English push inland from Virginia and the Atlantic seaboard; the French sweep south on waterways from New France (Canada) to control fertile deltas of the Mississippi River and its vast lower valley. And the Spanish string their gold-and-gospel trails and Catholic church missions through the Southwest and along the Pacific Coast of California.

In the 1680s, hastened by the French on the Mississippi seeking a Gulf colony to curb the Spanish, the viceroy of New Spain hastily authorizes eleven maritime expeditions to locate and destroy intruders from French Canada. Robert Cavalier de la Salle's voyage down the Mississippi to its mouth confirms French ambitions.

Enrique Barroto is among Spanish captains seeking the elusive La Salle—a futile effort since the French colonist and his followers had not been where the Spanish thought and had perished at Matagorda Bay in Texas. Exploring the eastern Gulf Coast, Barroto's talented seaman, Juan Jordan de Reina, rediscovers the sought-after harbor, noting in his journal on

French colonist Pierre le Moyne de Iberville who established settlements west of Pensacola near Biloxi.
Colonial Mobile *by Peter J. Hamilton*

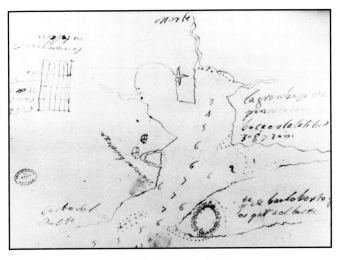

Jaime Franck's 1698 map of Pensacola Bay indicates the site of Fort San Carlos de Austria which was located near present Fort Barrancas and the proposed fort at Point Siquenza on Santa Rosa Island, not built until 1719.
Pensacola Historical Society

February 6, 1686, "about 11 o'clock I saw a bay, the best I have ever seen in my life . . . the Indians call this bay Panzacola . . . With the Indian pilot we went in the longboat to the village of the Panzacola . . ."

Jordan de Reina reports the Panzacolas friendly; the natives want trade goods and fear being decimated by the stronger Mobile settlements. Thereafter the Spanish pilot envisions colonization of the valued harbor—an adventure favored by Spaniards in Vera Cruz, including Andres de Pez, a captain of the Windward Squadron. Pez, leader of three of the voyages in search of the feared French, enlists support from New Spain's leading mathematician and scientist, Dr. Carlos de Siguenza y Gongora, who learns of the harbor from his former student Barroto. Pez petitions the newly arrived viceroy, the Conde de Galve, to colonize what Luna had named Santa Maria harbor. He so favors the Gulf Coast harbor he recommends moving the St. Augustine settlers and blocking the St. Augustine harbor. His boldness stirs controversy and rejection by the Madrid war council. Nonetheless, in 1689 Pez is ordered to Spain for resolution.

After almost four years of debate, Charles II sets aside the council's decision and orders the Pez expedition, except for abandonment of St. Augustine. Yet the unenthusiastic council wins a compromise: the king's cedula of June 26, 1692, orders another scientific examination of the bay, with the viceroy authorized to build defenses if expedient.

For the survey, the Conde de Galve chooses Pez, now an admiral; and Pez, accompanied by Jordan de Reina and Siguenza, reaches the harbor on April 7, 1693, proclaiming it for the king and re-christening it Bahia de Santa Maria de Galve—honoring the viceroy while retaining the sacred name chosen by Luna.

Siguenza finds the Luna description valid and recognizes the harbor's La Barranca, or Barrancas Colorados (Red Cliffs) as a strategic point. He muses "this was the very port found by a pilot named Miruelo shortly after the discovery of America . . . this was the port called Ochuse which Captain Maldonado sought and found."

He attaches his own name to the western point of the Isle de Santa Rosa, Siguenza Point, and calls the opposite mainland point San Carlos—both adaptable for defenses guarding the harbor entrance. The bank itself—probable location of the Luna settlement—he names Barranca de Santo Tome.

Returning to Mexico, the survey party is enthusiastic for fortification and settlement. And by now Admiral Pez envisions a La Florida governorship.

Despite the June 3, 1694 cedula ordering the viceroy to begin colonization, court politics, lack of money and passing of principal players from the scene obscure the expedition. Galve dies in 1695, Siguenza suffers poor health and Admiral Pez, ambitions shattered, is in disrepute.

Yet, in 1697, with France again moving swiftly to settle the Gulf, the Spanish war council acts with equal dispatch, making fortification of Bahia de Santa Maria de Galve urgent priority for the empire. If the Spaniards want La Florida, they must sail; and to Don Andres de Arriola—reluctant from the start—and Dr. Siguenza fall the planning for the arduous task of colonizing the harbor as an effective barrier against the French and British.

Two years earlier, clearing the Gulf of troublesome pirates, Arriola had visited Santa Maria harbor; he's not enthusiastic for the mission, specially for sailing in the autumn season on a venture not entirely popular. Besides, when he sets sail from Vera Cruz with about 350 soldiers, his colonists are mostly convicts, beggars, and other dregs of society pressed into service.

But he does not sail alone. Juan Jordan de Reina, then in Spain, hurries to Havana, requisitions troops and supplies, and sails for the northern Gulf harbor.

Arriving in November 1698, Arriola's Vera Cruz expedition finds Captain Jordan, who had preceded him by four days on one of the two sloops from Havana, already constructing the outpost on the red-clay Barranca Santo Tome, later the site of American-built Fort Barrancas.

Sixty-year-old Austrian engineer Jaime Franck, famed as the best military planner in the New World, and now awaiting retirement, is pressed into service to design and build the pine-log fortification Arriola names Fort San Carlos de Austria. Within a week the colonizers—a few friars, 350 infantrymen, and a labor battalion of black convicts—are living in palmetto-thatched huts and manning a harbor gun battery.

Arriola has a foothold, but the feared French are on a near horizon.

Two months later, Pierre le Moyne de Iberville, sailing from Brest, anchors his five-ship French expedition off Santa Maria harbor. But Arriola refuses entry, causing uneasy hours for the small Spanish garrison before Iberville sails west to establish a colony near Biloxi and begin French fortunes in what would become Louisiana and control of the Mississippi valley with settlements from Mobile to New Orleans.

Fort San Carlos de Austria was named for Charles or Carlos, fourteen, second son of Leopold I, emperor of Austria, and pretender to the Spanish throne. The wooden fort with sand-filled bastions and parapets mounts eighteen cannon—eight-pounders and ten-pounders—peering out from the sandy crest of the bluff. Building it is a miserable task for Franck, reporting during his sixty years he "had never seen such a sorry job, shoved into a wretched hut always in a danger of fire." And fire strikes often, leveling the structure. Worse, Franck moans, "is the quality of this presidio whereby the jails and junk shops of Mexico had been cleaned out." Moreover, he rightly predicts desertions, with settlers going to live with the Indians or returning home.

The coastal weather—strong winds, constantly shifting sands—undermines the structure, and by the early 1700s the logs are rotting. Fort commander Don Francisco Martinez says the shabby place consists "solely of a quadrangle of logs which would serve only as a stepping-over place for the enemy."

But settlers erect other buildings, including a hospital staffed by two surgeon friars, just in time for an epidemic which decimates the population in 1702. Franck sees the futility and waste of funds of the royal treasury—hostility of the Indians, poor quality of the soil, unbearable climate. He quarrels the place will shorten the days of those who live in such climate.

The Spaniards find their exile a place of horror. Confined to austere solitude, the subsidized presidio lacks basic provisions, and resorts to convict labor, friendly Indians, mulattoes, blacks, and trade with French Mobile. Daily food is a ration of eight ounces of bread or corn and meat seasoned with salt water; sometimes bitter acorns and tree roots. No women are in the 1698 expedition; by 1713, only twenty-five females receive subsidies.

With the Spanish allied with the French in the War of Spanish Succession (1702-1713), only the stronger French Mobile garrison helps lessen fears of British-led marauding Indians, attacking Panzacola frequently. Still, the Upper Creeks burn the Pensacola garrison in 1707. And—foreshadowing events to come—the English Union Jack flies momentarily over Santa Maria de Galve presidio until the peace treaty.

Yet the Spanish hold, despite rotting timbers, fleas, and pervasive heat weakening the fort and garrison.

Maintenance is hampered by shifting sand and limited fresh water; gun batteries lack power to deter ships from entering the harbor. Repeated pleas to relocate to Santa Rosa Island bring only a small battery to Siquenza Point in 1719.

Meanwhile, unknown to the presidio, Spain and France are again at war in Europe. And the Mobile French, led by Jean Baptiste Le Moyne and his brother, the Sieur de Bienville, sail an expedition into the bay May 14, 1719, surprising the Spanish. They exchange shots with Fort San Carlos. The French invaders seize the dunes above the fort, and Governor Juan Pedro Matamoras surrenders the Spanish settlement of 370 people.

Another Bienville brother, Lemoyne de Chateague, becomes Panzacola commandant, moving in 250 troops, heightening French dreams of establishing the capital of French Louisiana at Panzacola. But the confident French, transporting the entire Spanish garrison to Cuba in French ships, according to surrender terms, sail into a Havana trap. The Cuban governor orders the French vessels seized and crews jailed as prisoners of war.

When New Spain learns of the French seizure, an expedition of 1,200 troops is quickly organized to counterattack. Using the two French ships as decoys, the Spanish sail easily into Panzacola Bay with demands for French surrender.

At first they refuse; after two days bombardment, largely effective, the French agree.

Now on alert, realizing the French will return, the Spanish strengthen the battery on Point Siquenza, and construct a small stockade to protect Fort San Carlos from land attack.

But again, in September, the French return, recapturing the fort. And, even though European peace is restored in 1720, the French retain sovereignty until 1722 when the treaty returns Panzacola to Spain. Under the treaty, with both countries allied against Great Britain, France renounces forever Panzacola claims. The last Frenchman leaves in 1723.

But the cautious French, in a defensive measure, leave a bitter legacy, blowing up the fort and leaving the village in ashes. Only the fort's bake oven and lidless cistern remain, and now the worrisome shifting sand will bury all traces of the often-burned, tormented Fort San

Carlos de Austria.

Rebuilding, the Spanish finally get their wish—opportunity to settle on Santa Rosa Island. Lt. Col. Alejandro Wauchope, heeding orders from superiors, constructs a new fort at Punta de Siquenza. Outer buildings represent a new town. By 1723, the stockage and town consist of thirty-five buildings, including a paymaster's office, two barracks, a house for the captain, powder magazine, twenty-four small buildings, eight larger homes, a cook oven, and a lookout tower.

In 1743, the first commercial cargo of timber—masts of yellow pine—and naval stores is exported by the Havana Company, foretelling an industry on the distant horizon. And Dom Serres of the Havana Company sketches the only known view of the island settlement, an illustration published in London in 1746.

Finally, the Spanish build a small fortification, San Miguel, on the bayfront mainland as protection for Christian Indians. Its location is present-day Seville Square.

Again, anger from the Gulf is deadly; howling hurricane winds in November 1752 strike the island settlement, leaving only two buildings standing. Yet, the determined Spanish, leaving administrative government at Punta de Siquenza, move to San Miguel. Already a financial drain on the royal treasury, the forlorn settlement—reduced to sixty militiamen and twenty-four laborers by the middle of the eighteenth century—is endangered by abandonment as officials debate its fate for four years.

But by 1757, the entire colony and fort are relocated, causing the new viceroy, Marques de las Amarillas, to authorize a new town and presidio, which he names San Miguel de las Amarillas. But King Ferdinand VII—invalidating the viceroy's usurpation of his authority—officially christens the settlement Presidio San Miguel de Panzacola on December 23, 1757. Even though known as the Province of Panzacola since 1698, the name is now official; only the spelling changes.

Inside the log-encircled stockade, the Spanish plan a church, hospital, government house, storehouse, bake oven, barracks for troops and a labor battalion, and houses for civilians and married officers and soldiers.

Yet another storm batters the mainland in 1760, washing away remnants of the crippled island community. Once more Panzacola undergoes rigors of a beleaguered frontier outpost, doomed to austere isolation. Nonetheless the bayfront settlement foretells its permanence—a Gulf Coast pawn for Spanish and English rivals.

Florida is not profitable for Spain; its natural wealth hidden and difficult to exploit. Besides, Spain lacks the population to colonize and short-sightedly prohibits immigration of foreigners and restricts migrating its own non-Catholic citizens to increase available manpower.

Spain simply could not hold the undeveloped and underpopulated Florida settlements when another storm brews—this one international: Spain enters the war against England, promptly losing Cuba to British forces. Under the 1763 Treaty of Paris, which reshapes North America, Spain ransoms Cuba by abandoning La Florida, ceding all possessions east of the Mississippi to the British.

France withdraws by delivering all territory except Louisiana, later given to Spain. But the Spaniards believe the forced cessions are temporary expedients. Spain retires from La Florida, determined to await the opportunity to reclaim the colony. For more than half a century, Florida, her permanent ownership in doubt, remains a pawn for those gambling the fate of imperialism.

But now the English, envisioning a Southern empire, have their first royal territory west of the Appalachian Mountains in the aftermath of the French and Indian War. And as the British Union Jack rides the heated Gulf air off Santa Rosa Island in August 1763 the Indian word *Panzacola*—spelled Pensacolle by the French—seeps into the language as *Pensacola*. Dreamers in far away London see their new possession at once a Garden of Eden and raw, brutal colonies expanding their North American frontier.

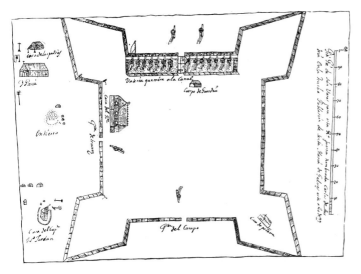

San Carlos de Austria in 1699.
Colonial Mobile *by Peter J. Hamilton*

The Spanish settlement on Santa Rosa Island was sketched by Don Serres who lived there in 1743. The sketch was originally published in the Universal Magazine, London, 1746. Pensacola Historical Society

A replica of the Santa Rosa Island village was built during the 1959 quadricentennial celebration. It has since been demolished. Pensacola Historical Society

George Johnstone (1730-1787) served as the first governor of British West Florida from 1764 until 1767. Pensacola Historical Society

2

A Royal Wilderness

Straight from victory over the Spanish in Havana, seeing spoils won in the Seven Years war, British occupation troops enter Pensacola August 6, 1763. They find only disappointing neglect on the edge of wilderness.

Not yet recovered from a torrid, feverish Caribbean campaign, 350 veteran Redcoats of the Third Battalion of the Royal American Regiment of Foot march into a crude settlement with their fiery crosses of Saint Andrew and Saint George replacing the descending lion and castle of the Spanish banner.

The regimental commander, Lt. Col. Augustine Prevost, accepts the outpost from Spanish Governor Diego Ortiz Parilla, who departs a month later with 700 settlers, including about 108 Yamasee Indians, for Havana and Vera Cruz.

Prevost criticizes the departing Spaniards for "insufferable laziness," leaving the country uncultivated, scrubby woods bearding the forlorn village.

Even frontier-hardened soldiers are astonished. Storm-wracked, dilapidated, the outpost consists of about one hundred huts and hovels encircled by a rotting stockade. The British characterize the fort as a half-mile of ground in circumference surrounded with a shabby stockade without a ditch, so defenseless anyone could step in at pleasure. Barracks are miserable bark huts.

But the British, lacking respect for the commercial acumen of the Spaniards, typical of the eighteenth century, have visions of profitable Indian trade and plantations enlivening a new commercial empire.

Under the Proclamation of 1763, the old French area along the Gulf is joined to Spanish Florida; the almost virgin territory from the Atlantic to the Mississippi is divided into West and East Florida. With Pensacola the capital, Royal West Florida extends along the Gulf to the Mississippi, up to the mouth of the Yazoo, due east to the Chattahoochee and down the Apalachicola to the Gulf. The almost rectangular colony encompasses the present Florida Panhandle, southern Alabama and Mississippi, and southeastern Louisiana.

With the brown Apalachicola, the Floridas' largest river snaking through swamps west of Apalachee, the divider, Pensacola and West Florida look to Mobile and the Mississippi Valley; East Florida with St. Augustine the capital is Atlantic in thought and interest.

Yet when the British arrive only Pensacola and Mobile are significant settlements, with Pensacola largely dependent on French neighbors for support.

The British proclamation calls for quieting the Indians by reassuring them of their lands and the administration and defense of the imperial domain.

Under the first civil governor, George Johnstone, contentious and aggressive Scotsman and Royal Navy officer, West Florida because of its frontier character is organized as a Parliament-subsidized royal colony; the Crown appoints the governor, upper-house council and judiciary and pay their salaries, and male voters elect the lower house, called the Assembly. But from the start, with the civil government jousting with military commanders, the colony is beset by conflict. London subsidies free citizens of taxes and the governor of dependence on the elected lower house—a factor keeping West Florida loyal to the Crown when American Whigs try to liberate the English possessions.

Speculative fever grips planters, merchants, destitute European immigrants, powerful British lords, and veterans of the Seven Years' War. But there are enough vacant acres in the Floridas for anyone willing to settle.

Johnstone moves quickly, overturns Spanish land grants and stabilizes relations with the intractable Choctaws, Chickasaws, and Creeks by reassuring them of land. By reallocating land sold by the Spanish before they departed, Johnstone and the council set in motion Pensacola's first townscape, designed by provincial surveyor Elias Durnford. In 1765 Durnford shapes the town around the old San Miguel stockade, renamed Fort of Pensacola. Durnford's Old City is still platted on city maps—the area encompassing Pensacola's first historical preservation district centering on Seville Square, established in 1967, 202 years later.

Setting aside governmental lands for the fort, barracks, public buildings, and streets, Durnford divides the balance into lots 80 by 160 feet, providing each property owner with a garden plot bordering a small stream on the northern edge of the community—prelude to aptly named Garden Street. Uniform-width streets named George, Charlotte, York, Gloucester, Cumberland, Mansfield, Johnstone, and Lindsey are at right angles—the plat basically unchanged in the Seville preservation district today, except for Spanish names.

The British bring the first substantial improvements from Pensacola to the Mississippi. But in unpopulated Panhandle Florida trails from the ruins of old Spanish Apalachee missions thread for more than one hundred miles. Crossing the Escambia River upstream, settlers follow high bluffs of the west bank; the river gradually widens, emptying into Pensacola Bay. Across the province, mostly west of Pensacola and Mobile, new towns are surveyed; scattered plantations begin. Campbell Town, near the mouth of the Escambia River, settled by French Protestant refugees, never prospers and is finally deserted. Most population centers on the Mississippi, with the rise of Manchac, site of British Fort Bute, Baton Rouge, and Fort Panmore on a high Natchez bluff—one of the most remote outposts of British America. By the 1770s, with a steady stream of war veterans arriving in the Mississippi area, approximately one-tenth of British military forces stretched out from Quebec and Montreal to the Gulf are stationed in the Floridas.

Traders travel by canoe and pack horse into the back country bartering imported goods and rum for deerskins, indigo, sawed lumber, corn, rice, hides, and fur. As a seaport, soldiers, sailors, emigres from sister colonies, blacks, Indians, and women congregate along streets. Despite Anglican hopes for a church, there are only occasional services by a Mobile minister. John Friby is schoolmaster, but he has no school. Merchants, the key leaders, gather for business and pleasure along wharves and in countinghouses and taverns, wearing plain waistcoats of striped cotton and Indian boots. Women dress lightly—reflecting the frontier lifestyle.

Despite being the capital and military command garrison, Pensacola is isolated. Besides bickering between civil governors and military leaders, soldiers grumble about food, housing, climate, boredom. The packet boat running between Pensacola, Jamaica, and Charleston is often late, feeding feelings of isolation and neglect. Yet pleasantries include bathhouses, billiard parlors, plays staged by officers in the garrison, shops vending hardware, clothing, tobacco, silverware, and books. Even bawdy houses make life more bearable. From the tower atop the governor's stone palace inside the rectangular wooden stockade sentries see pine forests greening sandy soil.

With the outbreak of the American Revolution, the military character of West Florida accelerates: English soldiers with heavy Brown Bess muskets, red woolen coats and freshly tarred black gaiters, kilted Scotsmen, and bitter Tory refugees organize into provincial units. German mercenaries, armed black slaves, and painted Indians with muskets and knives are more numerous. Along with hundreds of sailors ashore, they discourage any West Floridian tempted to speak up for George Washington and the Continental Congress. American Whigs never succeed in liberating West Florida. Spain will.

Pensacola civil authorities reflect the colony's instability. The bellicose, bickering Johnstone, whose Indian policies mark his only success, is finally removed; his successor, John Elliot, hangs himself one month after arriving in Pensacola.

Conflicts subside with the arrival of the last governor, Peter Chester, in 1770. Chester, who refrains from feeding the civil-military argument and tries for self-sufficiency by encouraging more settlers, follows the military tradition of predecessors Johnstone, Monfort Browne, Elliot, and Durnford, all officers in King George's armed forces.

In 1774, Durnford reports approximately 4,900 people—including 2,500 blacks—living in the colony, with less than a thousand in Pensacola.

But by Chester's administration, the War for American Independence is on the horizon; west of the Mississippi the Spanish are renewing ambitions for reclaiming West Florida holdings.

Resistance in the Thirteen Colonies to the north fails to arouse West Floridians, who prefer independence; they pass up the Continental Congress and ignore the English prohibition against trading with rebellious Americans.

Many Tories seek safe haven, and by 1775 Governor Chester provides land grants for hundreds of Loyalists from every colony arriving in the lower Mississippi River valley.

Americans periodically attack West Florida shipping in the Gulf, and Chester fears an overland attack. Pensacola is strategically important, and a war scare causes a flurry of defensive activity in the poorly prepared capital. Fortifications are in disrepair as the Spanish—working diligently with the Americans for support of the Indians—feed threats of war along the Mississippi frontier.

Capt. James Willing's American raiders strike deep in the lower Mississippi valley in 1778, prompting English Gen. Henry Clinton to order regular troops, German mercenaries, and other Loyalist forces to the Gulf Coast under command of Gen. John Campbell. For more than a year, Campbell works against great odds—without funds or credit, vessels, materials, officers, or engineers—strengthening the old Pensacola stockade and erecting new defenses.

The British build the Royal Navy Redoubt on

Elias Durnford surveyed Pensacola and designed a town plan which provided for a central military section flanked by a grid of residential streets beyond which were garden plots. Pensacola Historical Society

Rebecca Durnford, wife of British surveyor Elias Durnford. Pensacola Historical Society

the Red Cliffs fronting the harbor entrance, and erect the Prince of Wales Redoubt, Queen's Redoubt, and Fort George on Gage Hill. General Campbell is confident, should the enemy ever breach the stockade fort below, his Redcoats can be masters of Gage Hill.

But the test comes not from rebellious Americans, but a young, dashing, determined, energetic Spanish nobleman named governor and captain-general of Louisiana in 1777—Bernardo de Galvez.

Still unhappy over losses to Great Britain, especially with the English entrenched in West Florida, Spain is alarmed by the threats to her Gulf possessions—the British enticing Louisiana inhabitants to migrate to West Florida, monopolizing Mississippi valley trade and encouraging Indian support in Spanish territory. On June 21, 1779, Spain declares war against England, and the brilliant Galvez wins the Mississippi valley in late 1779. Attacking from New Orleans August 27 with about five hundred troops, Field Marshal Galvez within a month gobbles up Fort Bute at Manchac, besieges Baton Rouge and accepts surrender of the British command, including the post of Natchez. By March 1780, Mobile is under the Spanish banner, and Galvez turns to his big prize and last stronghold—Pensacola and Fort George on Gage Hill.

On March 9, 1781, Galvez launches a sixty-one-day amphibious assault and land siege on Pensacola fortifications with the aid of French and Indian allies. The heterogeneous invasion is composed of Spanish grenadiers, French chasseurs, seamen, Louisiana Creoles, blacks, Belgians, Irishmen, Walloonians, Haitians, and Indians.

Landing on Santa Rosa Island, Galvez personally captains his fleet into the harbor under peril of British cannon and supervises the attack with 1,300 troops, eventually reinforced by 900 from Mobile and 1,400 from New Orleans.

Campbell musters 1,700 defenders—Maryland and Pennsylvania Loyalists, German mercenaries from the Province of Waldeck, West Florida Royal Foresters, Royal Navy seamen, blacks, local provincials called *crackers,* and native Creek, Choctaw, and Chickasaw Indians.

With an encircling movement, the Spanish invaders cross bayous and streams, skirmish with Loyalists and Indians and jockey for siege position against British fortifications. Shot in the hand and abdomen, the wounded Galvez is back in command as the invaders battle a month before coming up against Fort George.

Then, the night of May 7, 1781:

Flashes and flames from howitzers, mortars and cannon brighten the dark spring night, thunder of war rattling over Fort George, the two redoubts, batteries, tents, and thousands of troops.

After midnight, cannoneers slow their barrages, but the night is a din of bullets, grapeshot and fusillades hanging frightfully in the long darkness.

Then, at 8:30 in the morning of May 8, a howitzer grenade whistling over the trenches ignites a gunpowder magazine. Flames leap like red tongues along the parapet and the stockade, triggering loaded bombs, grenades, and barrels of powder in a gigantic deadly force dismembering men and tearing apart the half-moon fort.

Into the flaming rubble grenadiers and chasseurs charge in two columns, with an advance of attackers snuffing fires and guiding the assault on other bastions. From the gunports, desperate British defenders pepper the assault force with cracking musket fire. Distant batteries pour shot and more hell into the melee, lacerating the earth and crumbling the fort walls.

Spaniards and allies, bathed in blood and smoke, claw and climb determinedly across the body-laden hillside. They push through the fractured walls of the fort, battling Britishers with bayonet, ball and musket butt, hand-to-hand, grabbing glory inch by inch.

And then, at three o'clock, a white flag in the smoky haze of Fort George.

For Galvez, on horseback, watching from the distance, it's a surprise.

Now, as gunners step back and the fighting ceases, an officer on horseback from General Campbell's command post appears. His accompanying servant signals the end: he carries a white flag. The dejected officer brings a letter from Campbell asking for a twenty-four hours' suspension of hostilities to arrange formal surrender.

The Spanish have their final triumph; they control Pensacola again, and along with it the entire Gulf Coast, dooming the royal wilderness colony.

Following the formal surrender May 10, the English have safe passage to New York. Most civilians remain on the Gulf Coast and along the Mississippi River; and despite Spanish encouragement, few stay in Pensacola—which again becomes sanctuary for Loyalists fleeing from the north.

The Galvez victory ends forever British hopes of holding the Floridas, blocks safe English navigation of the vital Mississippi River, and terminates their under-defended sanctuary in the Gulf of Mexico.

For size and significance, the Battle of Pensacola is the largest for Florida and for the Gulf Coast, from the coming of the Spanish to Pensacola through the War of 1812 when Andrew Jackson's Americans defeat the British in the swamps of New Orleans for the last time on American soil. Although Spain and the eastern colonies are never authorized allies, the Galvez campaign keeps British troops focused on West Florida for more than a year—forces that could have reinforced Lord Charles Cornwallis in the main eastern theater of war. Loss of West Florida helps signal the final collapse of British fortunes in the New World. Events in Pensacola helped shorten the road to the Yorktown surrender field where Gen. George Washington's Continental Army and French allies basked in a pageant of victory banners before sullen, defeated Redcoats.

Galvez is the hero, promoted to lieutenant general; destined to govern New Spain as viceroy. Pensacola Bay is renamed *Bahia de Santa Maria de Galvez,* and the Galvez flagship, *Galveztown,* is emblazoned on his coat of arms with the inscription, *Yo Solo,* commemorating his personal courage leading the fleet into the bay under British guns of the Royal Navy Redoubt. A bronze sculpture of Galvez and symbolic Fort George Park southwest of Lee Square on Gage Hill commemorate the Battle of Pensacola, which spilled over what became the North Hill residential neighborhood, Pensacola's second preservation district designated for its Victorian wooden architecture during the city's turn-of-the-century lumber boom.

By 1783, conquered West Florida lands and East Florida are formally returned to the throne of Spain.

Peter Chester, last British governor of West Florida, served through the American Revolutionary War period. Pensacola Historical Society

British Pensacola in the late 1760s, as seen by cartographer George Gould, was published by Thomas Jeffrey in London in the 1770s.
Pensacola Historical Society

This 1770 plan of Pensacola was drawn by mapmaker Joseph Purcell.
Pensacola Historical Society

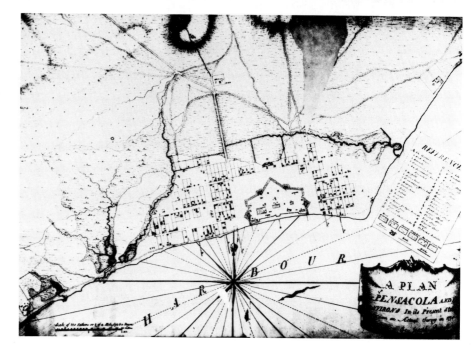

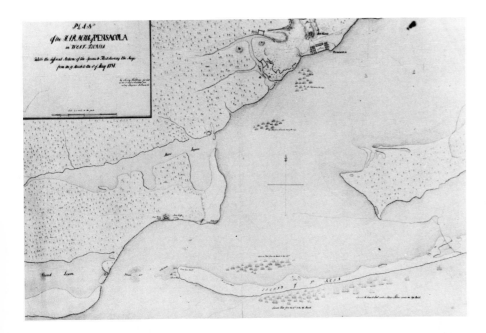

This plan of the 1781 Siege of Fort George and the redoubt on Gage Hill shows where Galvez's troops landed at the mouth of Sutton's Lagoon (Bayou Chico) and moved up to Galvez Springs where they constructed batteries to assault the Queen's Redoubt. *William Clements Library*

This famous view of the 1781 Battle of Pensacola shows Galvez on horseback in the foreground and the explosions in the Queen's Redoubt which brought the siege to an end. The engraving is by M. Ponce and M. Godefrey. *Pensacola Historical Society*

The Lavalle House, built by Charles Lavalle, builder and brickmaker between 1805 and 1815, is one of the oldest still surviving dwellings in Pensacola. Its architecture depicts the raised Creole cottage built with the Gulf Coast environment in mind; allowing for cross ventilation and free passage of flood waters from hurricanes and a cooling air flow beneath the building. *Pensacola Historical Society*

The Innerarity house at the site of the Panton Leslie and Company's well-known trading post was photographed in the 1890s.
Pensacola Historical Society

3

Twilight For Spain

Spreading almost a mile along the bay, and extending north about five blocks, wharves linking sea and sand, Pensacola in the 1780s retains its wilderness isolation known earlier by the founding Spanish. Yet the conquerors are content with British leavings, especially fortifications superior to those relinquished in 1763. They change only the names.

Poorly marked trails link Pensacola with its nearest wilderness neighbor—on the east, St. Marks; on the west, Mobile.

On the north, beyond battle-scarred Gage Hill—renamed Mount San Miguel—swamps and pine forests still crowd the remote outpost, or Plaza as it's known by the returning Spanish. A cypress-stake stockade encloses the governor's house, barracks for the garrison and several storehouses. Outside, two hundred porched wooden houses surrounded by wooden fences shape the British-built town.

The land rises gently from the bay (today's Main Street) to about present day Garden Street. Beyond, some seventy-nine feet above sea level, from the crest of Gage Hill where Galvez sealed West Florida's fate, two streams—Cadet's Spring and San Gabriel (Washerwoman's Bayou)—trickle east and west to the shore. San Gabriel empties in the bay west of Calle de Barcelonia; Cadet's Spring, flowing past the Spanish burial ground that becomes St. Michael's Cemetery, washes

through a swamp east of Calle de Cevallos. Natural boundaries, the swampy, spring-fed streams are sources for water and public laundering.

Despite return of the conquering Spanish, who regain official ownership with the 1783 Treaty of Paris, the town designed by Elias Durnford retains British characteristics. Wooden houses are one-and-a-half story, multi-room structures with piazzas and brick chimneys, and simple modest cottages of three rooms or less.

Suited to Southern seacoast climate, Creole structures in Pensacola are like those of New Orleans, Mobile, and Carribean areas where French reside. Yet, at the outset of the last Spanish period, wind still swirls sand of unpaved streets now known by a litany of melodious Spanish names.

The plaza, known as the "common," is bounded on the north of Calle de Nueva (Government Street), by Calle de Palafox to the west and Calle de Alcaniz on the east. Again life centers on the government district; inside the walled compound stand the two-story governor's house and garden, customs house, church and residence of the parish priest, jail (calaboza), several warehouses, barracks, and hospital.

When the flag changes, British settlers depart, replaced by Spaniards from Spanish Louisiana, Canary Islands, and from the French Creole populations of other Caribbean islands. They are mostly French, known for dancing and merry-making. By 1796, one third of the five hundred to six hundred residents are Negro and mulatto slaves.

Adding to the ethnic melting pot is Pensacola's first matriarch—French-born, skillful business-woman Marianna Bonifay, who arrives in 1784 and acquires a home on Calle de Intendencia. She joins neighbor Charles LaValle in the investment and construction of new Pensacola houses. His daughter, Maria Louise, marries Don Manuel Gonzalez, with Marianna providing a dowry of a slave girl and seven hundred pesos in Mexican coin. Gonzalez, with a grant from the Spanish crown, develops the Gonzalez ranch north of Pensacola on his three square-mile tract that will become known in the nineteenth and twentieth centuries as Cantonment. By the early 1800s, Marianna Bonifay and Charles LaValle are joint owners of Gaberone Point and operating brick kilns near the clay bluffs jutting up from Escambia Bay. Strong willed, profit-minded Marianna Bonifay not only pioneers the brick industry destined to flourish in the nineteenth century—her union with LaValle begins the many generations of Bonifay descendants continuing in the twentieth century. By the railroad-building era of the 1880s, the Holmes county seat, Bonifay, would continue the legacy of her family name; and her property today between Scenic Highway and the Pensacola Regional Airport is known as the Gaberone and Lavallet residential neighborhoods.

No longer living in a capital, now governed by the governor-general of Louisiana and West Florida based in New Orleans, the Spanish transform Pensacola, repairing its dilapidated fortifications.

British Fort George is renamed Fort San Miguel; the Prince of Wales battery becomes Fort Sombrero because the Spanish think its shapes resembles a hat; the Queen's Redoubt is repaired and named Fort San Bernardo in honor of Galvez.

Across the harbor, the Royal Navy Redoubt on the Barrancas, in poor condition, becomes Fort San Carlos de Barrancas. Nature begins erasing the Battle of Pensacola trenches, redoubts and batteries; Galvez's major encampment at Galvez Spring on Bayou Chico stands empty.

Settling down with the British-engineered townscape, the Spanish give Pensacola streets names that endure: George Street becomes Calle de Palafox, saluting Gen. Jose de Palafox y Melzi,

who defends Zaragoza, Spain, in the Peninsula War (1808-1809) and became the Duke of Zaragoza; Mansfield Street becomes Calle de Zaragoza, keeping alive memories of the Spanish city's valiant defense against Napoleon; Pitt and Bute streets are joined as Calle de Nueva (Government); Granby and Harcourt streets are merged as Calle de Intendencia for the Intendent or royal treasurer; Prince Street is retitled Calle de la Romana; Charlotte Street is changed to Calle de Alcaniz; Calle de Tarragona reflects the heritage of Catalonia, Spain; York Street becomes Calle de Floridablanca, honoring the Spanish junta president; Cumberland Street is renamed Calle de Baylen; Johnstone Street is designated Calle de Barcelonia; Lindsey Street becomes Calle de Reus; Gloucester Street is known as Calle de Cevallos.

Again, Spanish commandants—Arturo O'Neill (1781-1792) and Vicente Folch y Juan (1796-1811)—encounter difficulty maintaining West Florida fortifications, securing adequate troops, supplies, presents for Indian traders, and other governmental expenses. Soldiers from Cuban and Havana regiments and prisons enliven the "out of the way" garrison—consuming spirits and wine, entertaining promiscuous women, and spreading disease.

Men work as commercial fishermen, carpenters, sailors, shipwrights, shopkeepers, grocers, masons, barbers and bleeders, bricklayers, and bakers. Women are laundresses, scrubbing clothes by hand along the nearby streams; seamstresses, dressmakers, and domestic servants. Some ply the world's oldest profession, pleasuring lonely soldiers.

Budding industries—brickmaking, naval stores, sawn lumber—portend Pensacola's future. Commandant Folch owns part of two sawmills sixteen miles north in pineywoods on a branch of the Escambia River.

But it's a canny Scot, William Panton, who shapes Pensacola's economy and its continuing focus in Anglo-Spanish intrigue by moving his thriving Indian-trading enterprise—the Panton, Leslie and Company—from St. Augustine to Pensacola in 1785. Panton sees his future on the Gulf when, after the American Revolution, Pensacola replaces Charleston as the most important port for Southern Indian trade. And in the wilderness below the Ohio River are thousands of Indians who had attracted trains of packhorses before the American Revolution—Creek, Cherokee, Chickasaw, Seminole, Choctaw.

During the 1770s, Panton and three prominent merchants in Georgia, South Carolina, and East Florida—Thomas Forbes, John Leslie, and William Alexander—develop extensive trade with the Indians and favor with English officials. When the American Revolution threatens trade, the American-hating merchants organize in 1783 and win support from Spanish officials at St. Augustine and Pensacola. The Spanish, lacking merchants capable of managing the complex Indian trade and failing to produce marketable trade goods, embrace the Panton enterprise. They expect Panton, Leslie and Company to furnish goods to the Creek and Seminole, and other British merchants at Mobile and New Orleans to supply the Choctaw and Chickasaw. As Panton, Leslie and Company thrust westward from St. Augustine to St. Marks, Pensacola and Mobile, and eventually the Mississippi River, it takes over more and more of the Southern Indian trade and eventually all of it, passing legally through Spanish territory.

Panton's success is enhanced by a silent partnership with his friend, Creek Indian leader Alexander McGillivray, celebrated son of a Scottish planter/trader Lachlan McGillivray and French/Creek Indian Sehoy Marchand. Charleston-educated, the remarkable McGillivray—who accompanied Indians helping defend British Pensacola against the Galvez troops in 1781—skillfully protects the interests of the Creek Nation by maintaining delicate relationships with the Spanish officials through Panton. Holding rank of lesser chiefs of the Wind Clan, McGillivray convinces the Indians to trade almost exclusively with Panton, Leslie and Company. He shares Panton profits until 1788.

The tall, slender McGillivray, with dark, piercing eyes glaring from below an abnormally broad and high forehead, with the gravity of regal bearing, gains recognition as a Creek leader after his father flees to Scotland after the outbreak of the American Revolution. He helps align his people with the British, who commission him a colonel. Yet he's a pragmatist, dedicated to survival of the Creek Nation, now threatened by American encroachment from the Eastern Seaboard.

Protective of Creek lands for Creeks, McGillivray enters into a secret treaty with the United States in 1790, attaining the stars of an American brigadier general. He knows the fate of the Creek Nation depends upon the disputed boundary in North American between the Span-

The Innerarity house was painted by Emma Chandler, a Pensacola artist, circa 1893.
Pensacola Historical Society

The Calaboza or Old Spanish Jail as painted by Emma Chandler in the 1880s was located at the southwest corner of Alcaniz and Intendencia streets. It was here that Andrew Jackson jailed Jose Callava, the last Spanish governor and here also that Jonathan Walker was imprisoned.
Pensacola Historical Society

ish and Americans in the event existing trade routes with Great Britain are closed. Paid an annual $1,200 stipend as American brigadier, McGillivray nonetheless continues his liaison with Panton.

And in Pensacola, Panton's on the doorstep of a vast southeastern interior ripe for international trade. Sea routes to Pensacola's great bay provide Panton a direct link with the outside world and opportunity to dominate the Indian trade market with ships transporting goods to and from England.

In exchange for skins and credit, the Panton, Leslie Company builds a profitable enterprise based at Pensacola and San Marcos de Apalache (St. Marks) by providing guns, ammunitions, blankets, cotton cloth, beads and other manufactured goods to Indians in Mississippi and Alabama country and as far north as Chickasaw Bluffs (Memphis).

By the 1790s, Panton's three-storied brick mansion—Pensacola's most distinguished building, headquarters for Panton, Leslie and Company—dominates the bayfront. Valued at $14,074 in 1801, the mansion signifies Panton's affluence and reputation as Pensacola's wealthiest individual. In his tanyard and along his wharves, he employs eighty workmen and clerks handling shipments of skins and goods. A small fleet of ocean-going vessels plies between English ports and Pensacola. Smaller vessels serve coastal towns of St. Marks, Mobile, and New Orleans.

Panton agents operate truckhouses (stores) and trudge through wilderness—from the Florida peninsula to the Mississippi River and from the Gulf to Lookout Mountain, Tennessee—bartering for the Pensacola headquarters. Creeks trade deerskins for salt, transported to Pensacola from company salt pans in the Bahamas. In addition to cattlehides, some produced from Panton's own ranges near Pensacola, the company buys Indians' and trappers' deer, beaver, otter, wildcat, and wolf. Panton profits soar; critics claim some as high as 500 percent. Moreover, Panton—banker for Pensacola inhabitants—supplies the Pensacola garrison with meat, credit, and other provisions obtained cheaply from Indians repaying old debts.

Yet the fate of McGillivray, the highly respected and undisputed leader of the Creeks, symbolizes the changed character of the frontier, caught in intrigue between Spain and the United States for Creek economic resources. McGillivray's sudden 1793 death in Pensacola robs the Creeks

of their most talented leader. Buried with McGillivray is a fortune and a legacy—military rank from Americans and British and full Masonic honors.

Ironically McGillivray's death parallels decline of Indian trade, reduction of Spanish holdings, and the pressure of Americans, sweeping across the southeast, gobbling up land and igniting more international intrigue.

Two years later, the 1795 Pinckney's Treaty establishes the United States-Spanish West Florida boundary at the thirty-first parallel, placing most of the Panton, Leslie customers in U.S. territory, sharply marking decline of the company by the dawn of the nineteenth century.

In 1801, with William Panton dead at sea, the old Panton, Leslie holdings become the John Forbes and Company, with John and Thomas Forbes senior partners. Others connected with the company, James and John Innerarity, guide the destiny of the company after John Forbes retires in 1817. Yet Panton's death—coupled with the advancing Americans—reduces the effectiveness of the firm as an instrument of Spanish Indian policy.

As nations angrily debate Southern boundaries, and pirates and smugglers along the Gulf make the status of vessels of various nations uncertain, Pensacola is caught in more intrigue. By 1802, Pensacola's population is 650, swelled by free mulattoes. Spain cedes Louisiana to France, and in 1803 the United States purchases Louisiana from Napoleon, claiming all lands west of the Perdido River. Hundreds of Spanish military and civilians flee eastward from American territory, crowding Pensacola—once again the colonial capital—with almost 1,400 people. Formerly dependent on New Orleans, Pensacola is now a province in its own right—in effect inheriting the position of New Orleans, including transfer of the Regiment of Louisiana.

In 1804 the Spanish colony attempts to bar Americans from West Florida, and Governor Vicente Folch y Juan legalizes the general commerce with the colonists in which the Panton, Leslie Company's monopoly is substantially modified.

A year later, President Thomas Jefferson's offer to buy West Florida is refused. And England, realizing Spain's hold on Florida was slipping, twice sends an American Loyalist, William Augustus Bowles—a Maryland regimental ensign who served in the British garrison at Pensacola when Spain captured it in 1781—into Florida to

John Innerarity, one of the successors
to John Forbes and Company, inheritors
of the Panton, Leslie and Company.
Pensacola Historical Society

rally the Creeks and Seminoles and subsequently the Cherokees, Chickasaws, and Choctaws.

The uprooted British Loyalists, with the Creeks electing Bowles "Director General" of the "State of Muskogee," operating from sanctuaries along the Ochlockonee River, had hoped to make the Southeast a British protectorate or colony. In April 1800, Muskogee had declared war on Spain, and Bowles' troops force the surrender of St. Marks, but the Spanish retaliate. Little more than a nuisance and embarrassment, the flamboyant Bowles—twice captured—nonetheless reveals the waning Spanish imperial power. Bowles dies in Cuba's Morro Castille in 1805.

Transfer of the government from New Orleans to Pensacola and greater freedom of trade encourages internal improvements. Eighty houses rise from the street paralleling the bay. In 1810 population is 1,000 and growing; three years later the census counts 3,063—mostly French Creoles, Scots, and Irish. Yet the quiet life in Pensacola reflects marked prosperity. Fishermen and gardeners produce food; butchers prepare beef bought from Indians.

The Governor's House becomes a barracks for troops; a large warehouse near the bayfront—formerly filled with the English king's stores—becomes a Catholic Church. Here, near the bay, a series of Catholic clerics, chief among them Father Santiago (James) Coleman, an Irishman, ministers Catholic residents and diligently—though less successfully—tries to save the souls of Protestants and friendly Indians during the formative years of the San Miguel Parish.

Along Calle de Zaragoza, the octagonal Tivoli dance hall and other public rooms of the Plaza are animated by some Spaniards' lust for gaming and womanizing.

A brickyard on the opposite side of the bay produces tiles and bricks. Residents buy American homespun cotton in stores; black women peddle goods from baskets. Yet there are no printers, potters, tinsmiths, coppersmiths, watchmakers, hatters, or saddlers.

By 1814, garden plots designed by Durnford to go with town lots are subdivided and sold at public auction. Increased population causes helter-skelter home construction and the large Plaza is dismantled, leaving two public squares that endure. The Palafox common is variously named for King Ferdinand VII and the Constitution of 1812; eastward the other square becomes Seville.

Social life centers on the governor's wife; ladies in short sleeves and trainless dresses mimic the French fashion scene. Men frequent taverns and billiard rooms; churchgoers find their state religion—Roman Catholic—in the old warehouse until the American Catholics build the first San Miguel parish church where Old City Hall stands today. Parishioners include Irish, French, Spaniards, Scots, and blacks.

Knowing their colony was again invaluable, the Spanish by 1793 develop a plan for Pensacola Bay defenses—a battery at Point Siquenza on the western tip of Santa Rosa Island, a water-level battery at the mainland Barrancas, and a fort above the battery to protect it from land attack.

In 1798 the water-level Battery San Antonio, started in 1793, is complete, and work is progressing on renovation of San Carlos de Barrancas, although lack of funds forbids a new and larger fortification.

More and more Americans crowd the town, mingling with Spanish settlers, signalling the lengthening shadow of American expansionism. The rising tide of the frontier is symbolized by the 1810 rebellion of Americans and a few Spaniards in the Baton Rouge district who proclaim the Republic of West Florida and hoist a lonestar flag. Settlers rebel against restrictions on self-government, land speculation, and religious freedom. The revolt rocks Pensacola with fears of subversion and rebellion spreading east of the Pearl River. But it's short-lived; American troops occupy the territory under the assumption American lives and property must be protected since the region was American under the Louisiana Purchase.

President James Madison asserts U.S. claims to West Florida to the Perdido, but Americans only occupy the territory to the Pearl.

And now in Pensacola, British agents supply the Creeks with guns and ammunition. And soon Creek Indians, wearing British uniforms, drill in the streets, and British agents—exploiting Spanish weakness—offer rewards for scalps of Americans. The political change inflames the frontier and launches the meteoric rise of a Tennessee backwoodsman with a British saber scar on his gaunt face—Andrew Jackson. Josiah Quincy typifies the American push south. "We want West Florida," he says. "By God, we will take West Florida."

And so they will. Andrew Jackson, riding out of the Southern scrub, destiny at his side, hating Spanish and English, knows West Florida will be American.

The Tivoli High house built by Juan Baptiste Cazenave in 1805, was destroyed in 1935.
Pensacola Historical Society

The Tivoli High house was reconstructed by the Historic Pensacola Preservation Board as a 1976 Bicentennial project.
Pensacola Historical Society

*Andrew Jackson, soldier and states-
man and provisional governor of the
Floridas in 1821.*
Pensacola Historical Society

P A R T

4

Andy Jackson's Frontier

Wilderness fields north of Pensacola run red with blood.

With American ambitions for Southern expansionism, and War with Britain, Upper Creek warriors north of Pensacola—brandishing crimson war clubs—seek slaughter of encroaching settlers.

They follow warpath demands of Shawnee Chief Tecumseh, who in 1811 thunders south, exploiting his dream of a Great Lakes-to-Gulf confederation to stifle white infiltration into Indian lands. The great chief arouses the warring faction of the Creek Nation, the Red Sticks, so named for their crimson war clubs. Tecumseh even promises his Southern allies their weapons will be made available at Pensacola, St. Marks, and other Spanish ports.

President James Madison's declaration of war against England gives the Creeks their opportunity; they launch a general uprising. It was led by a half-blood nephew of the legendary Alexander McGillivray—William Weatherford, seven-eighths Creek, known as Chief Red Eagle by his mother's people, she being the half sister of McGillivray.

Andrew Jackson, now major general of Tennessee's ably trained twenty-five thousand volunteers, and a bellicose frontier nationalist, wants military fame and the American eagle flying over Mobile, Pensacola, and St. Augustine.

Jackson, the frontier's natural leader, is a planter, having been gambler, duelist, lawyer, Superior Court justice, and governor. He despises the British. In the American Revolution he sees most of his family die at the hands of the British. At age thirteen, the tall, agile, blue-eyed, freckle-faced boy of the North and South Carolina frontier serves as a mounted orderly, carrying messages for the Americans. Captured by the British, young Andy refuses a Redcoat officer's orders to clean his boots; the officer lifts his sword and aims. Jackson throws up his left arm, but the blade cuts to the bone and opens a gash on his head.

Jackson, heading for New Orleans, in 1813, wears many other scars. His narrow haggard face implies he's older than his forty-five years; his remarkably piercing eyes wear the fixed stare of a hawk, surmounting a bold shock of silvery hair as unruly as his hair-trigger temper.

He has a passionate devotion to Rachel, who had not been divorced when they first married and whose good name Jackson is ready to defend—and does—to the death, if need be.

He finds his military opportunity when the United States seizes upon the situation to claim all lands west of the Perdido River. He seeks to join Gen. James Wilkinson in defense of New Orleans against Southern invasion. President Madison also hopes to build a strike force that would seize eastern Florida and keep it after the war as reparation.

Jackson leaves Nashville by flatboat in January 1813 with frontier troops who hate Spaniards, Englishmen, and Indians and who know little and care less about international law. Yet their desire is stymied when Jackson is ordered to dissolve his division of volunteers at Natchez. The impetuous Jackson refuses, marching his troops back to Tennessee at his own expense, winning the sobriquet *Old Hickory*. And it's General Wilkinson—marching unopposed into Mobile, jolting the helpless Spanish commander to surrender without bloodshed—who completes American occupation of lands west of the Perdido River. The loss of Mobile shrinks Spanish holdings to Pensacola, St. Marks, and St. Augustine.

A renegade mixed blood, Peter McQueen, leads a thousand Indians to Pensacola demanding powder and ammunition, boasting of their lust for American blood. The fearful Spanish gladly oblige, and, on August 4, 1813, the Creek War begins when settlers clash with McQueen's Indians at Burnt Corn—eighty miles north of Pensacola. Terrified Alabama settlers abandon their homes, flee for defensible sanctuaries, including Ford Mims, the fortified residence of mixed-blood Samuel Mims on the Alabama River, thirty-five miles north of Mobile, then in Mississippi territory.

Red Eagle's braves surprise and slaughter settlers and Creeks in the Fort Mims massacre that alarms the frontier, accelerating the Creek War. In Pensacola, Spaniards watch Creeks parade 250 scalps from the Mims slaughter on war poles in the sand streets. And that's too much for Old Hickory. The Fort Mims butchery so angers Major General Jackson that he leaves his Nashville sickbed to rally a militia invasion force of two thousand Tennesseeans. Says Jackson, launching a whirlwind campaign against Creek strongholds, "By the eternal, these people must be saved."

He's finally on the road to Pensacola, New Orleans, and national fame.

Yet, all the while, Jackson's eyes are on Florida: *invade it, capture Pensacola, destroy the insidious influence of Spain, silent ally of Britain and open supporter of the rebellious Creeks.*

Still bloodstained with two gunshot wounds inflicted on him in a dispute over a friend's duel, Jackson delivers crushing defeats to the Creek Red Sticks along the Coosa and Tallapoosa rivers, destroying them at Taladaga and at Horseshoe Bend in March 1814. His three thousand men attack the fortified Tallapoosa River positions of the Creeks and their Cherokees allies, killing eight hundred; and the capitulation of the Indian raiders leads to the Treaty of Fort Jackson, opening twenty-three million acres of Alabama and Georgia land for American settlement.

When Creek renegades flee for sanctuary in Spanish Florida, Jackson slices south from Fort Jackson along the Coosa and Alabama rivers, pursuing Creeks and Seminoles, hewing a wilderness road for future American settlers. He pushes into occupied Mobile, and then strikes at the root of the problem—the English naval bases and Spanish defenses at Pensacola.

Spanish Governor Gonzales Manrique befriends the British. In August 1814, two English men-of-war appear in Pensacola Bay, putting ashore two hundred marines. Manrique allows Maj. Edward Nicholls and Capt. George Woodbine of the Royal Marines to occupy Fort San Miguel and Fort San Carlos de Barrancas as British garrisons, thereby violating Spanish neutrality. The British, arming Indians and enlisting runaway Negroes, promise Manrique to protect Pensacola from the Americans and pledge to restore Mobile and other Spanish territories to their former owners.

Along the march—fifteen miles north of Pensacola—Jackson seeks a guide to the Spanish defenses as his troops approach Vacaria Baja, cattle ranch of Don Manuel Gonzalez, an officer in the Spanish commissary department. Through an interpreter, Jackson minces no words: he wants Gonzalez's son, Celestino, to guide his army to Barrancas. When the prideful Don Manuel refuses, the angered Jackson threatens use of force.

But Don Manuel stands firm: "General, my life and my property are in your power; you can take both; but my honor is in my own best keeping. As to my son, I would rather plunge a sword into his bosom than see him a traitor to his king."

Surprised, Jackson extends his hand. "Sir, I honor a brave man."

He finds one Spanish friend, but for others in Pensacola Jackson is the invader.

By the afternoon of November 6, 1814, Jackson reaches Pensacola defenses. Under a flag of truce, Jackson sends his demands to Manrique: departure of the British and American occupation of Fort San Carlos de Barrancas, Fort San Miguel, and Santa Rosa until "Spain could preserve unimpaired her neutral character."

But the governor never receives the letter. Gunshots—probably British—shatter the flag of truce. And Jackson, with Biblical brimstone—"An Eye for an Eye, Tooth for Tooth and Scalp for Scalp"—launches his attack in four columns, three American and one Choctaw Indian, catching the Spanish completely by surprise. Storming the town from east and west, Jackson's troops race through the streets, driving Spanish soldiers from houses and gardens. Over in minutes, the speed of victory stuns Governor Manrique, who totters forward with a white flag of surrender.

Yet Jackson fumes over the delay of surrendering the forts, charging "Spanish treachery"—knowing he must now storm British-held Fort San Carlos de Barrancas.

But he's spared the task on the morning of his planned assault when he hears the British explode the Santa Rosa battery, demolish Fort San Carlos and adjoining village, and spike Battery San Antonio guns. A column of smoke rises from the Barrancas, leaving the harbor defenseless. Reeling from Jackson's threat, the British retreat to their ships, sailing for English strongholds on the Apalachicola River with several hundred Indians and runaway Negro slaves. Left with wreckage of the fort, Jackson finds "the satisfaction to see the whole British force leave the post and their friends at our mercy."

Jackson finds no temptation to hold the fort or remain in Pensacola, since the town is defenseless against future British attack. For strategic reasons, he returns Pensacola to Governor Manrique. Believing his mission a total success, he tells James Monroe he has "broken up the hot bed of the Indian war" and convinces Spaniards that the United States would no longer tolerate violations of neutrality jeopardizing American safety. He then returns to Mobile.

His actions, though not authorized, prove strategically sound; had he not conquered the Creeks, the British at Mobile and Pensacola could have used their coastal bases to invade the United States and then across to the Mississippi.

Besides, the British are now soured by ineptitude and indecision of Spanish Pensacolians. And the Spanish are horrified by the English, who kidnap almost all of the slaves in Pensacola and liberate other property; they want nothing more to do with the British. And Jackson's invasion diminishes Indian desire to aid the British.

So if the British keeps a toehold on the Floridas, they must do it alone.

On his return to Mobile, Jackson learns Nicholls has established a fort on the Apalachicola River—obviously a staging area for raids on the frontier settlements of Georgia as well as a point of attack on Fort Jackson to cut off American supplies from the Alabama area.

But Florida must wait. Keeping an eye on the Florida provinces, Jackson's off to New Orleans for an electrifying victory over the Redcoats, giving the young republic a psychological lift—even though the Treaty of Ghent is signed, but not ratified by the Senate. And Jackson doesn't know the War of 1812 has ended when his Tennesseans fight to victory in Chalmette Plantation swamps.

Jackson, now the nation's greatest hero since George Washington, solidifies his new national eminence by keeping active in West Florida, the focus of expansionists.

But as Spain struggles to control its Florida provinces, fearing Jackson's guns, beleaguered Pensacola suffers, trade dwindles, some settlers depart; others embrace Americans already settling along the Escambia River. Only remnants of the Regiment of Louisiana remain, largely ineffective, aided by a handful of Negro and mulatto troops. By 1816, population falls to five hundred; two years later—when Jackson again claims the Spaniards are harboring Indians—it drops to four hundred persons. It's now obvious Spain cannot hold Pensacola and protect its citizens.

With Pensacola in the middle, the Spanish provinces in outline resemble a massive pistol—the butt the peninsula of East Florida; the trigger guard the Apalachicola River valley; the barrel, a long strip of land slicing under Mississippi and Alabama, pointing menacingly at the Mississippi, the most coveted commercial artery in North America.

In the eyes of Secretary of State John Quincy Adams and Jackson, the provinces are filled with hostile Indians, runaway slaves, foreign adventurers, and duplicitous Spanish officials.

Renegades continue supplying and arming the British-built Negro Fort on Prospect Bluff of the Apalachicola, a river refuge for Indians and runaway slaves terrorizing Georgia border settlements. Aided by unauthorized British soldiers, Seminoles and Creeks raid border settlements in the Battle of Fowltown, shattering Jackson's

Treaty of Fort Jackson. Americans chase the Indians deeper into the Florida swamps; more settlers move their cabins south. As Indian raiders retaliate, Jackson launches his second expedition into West Florida in 1818, allegedly over treaty violations, but the James Monroe administration probably encouraged the second invasion, in part, to facilitate American expansion in Florida.

From Fort Scott near the border, Jackson moves swiftly, driving the Seminoles before him, burning their villages, establishing his base at the Prospect Bluff fort, which he renames Fort Gadsden for his engineer and aide, Capt. James Gadsden, and marches east. He seizes the St. Marks fort, hoisting the Stars and Stripes; marches to the Seminole town of Chief Billy Bowlegs on the Suwannee, attacks the fleeing Indians and burns three hundred houses; then he accuses two British subjects, seventy-year-old Scotsman Alexander Arbuthnot and swaggering, roistering former Royal Marine Lt. Robert Ambrister, of aiding the Indians. For Jackson, aiding Indians meant massacring Americans. Convicted by a drumhead court-martial, the two traders are put to death—Arbuthnot hanged at the end of the yardarm of his own ship; Ambrister shot, his head a mass of wounds.

The Indians, seeing the remains of their executed friends, sue for peace; they now see Jackson as a terrible, vindictive enemy against whom they find only their graves and confiscation of their property.

Returning to Fort Gadsden, Jackson notifies Secretary of War John C. Calhoun that he intends to march overland and strike Pensacola, center of Spanish rule where Indians have free access and are supplied with munitions of war. "Pensacola must be occupied with an American force," Jackson asserts, "the Governor treated according to his desserts or as policy may dictate."

Crossing the Apalachicola at Ocheesee Bluff May 7, 1818, Jackson's army trudges through the swampy, river-ribboned Alabama-Florida border country and then along the centuries-old Red Ground Creek Indian Trail, arriving on the northern shore of Escambia Bay May 24. The troops are mostly barefoot, with swampy trails first taking their horses and then their shoes.

The Spanish governor, Col. Jose Masot, hurls a series of warnings, promising repulsion by force. But Jackson easily brushes aside token resistance, captures the town, and concentrates forces on Masot's retreating forces inside Fort

San Carlos de Barrancas. Refusing Jackson's demand for surrender, Masot appeals for peace and friendship. Jackson responds by dragging forward his single nine-pound piece and five eight-pound howitzers and ordering the building of ladders to scale the walls. A slight puff of resistance fades quickly; the Spanish raise the white flag and march out in surrender. Masot, at least, demonstrates his loyalty to the king with one small gesture of defiance. Besides, Jackson is mistaken; there are no Indians massed in Pensacola.

Ever bombastic, wishing he had stormed the works and put the Spanish governor on trial for murder, Old Hickory nonetheless agrees to terms of capitulation. He allows the garrison to retire from the fortress with full honors of war and to transport the troops to Cuba. Moreover, he agrees to respect Spanish rights and property.

Jackson, promising respect for Spanish law, establishes a provisional Florida government with Col. William King of the Fourth Infantry appointed civil and military governor of Pensacola. He names Captain Gadsden collector with full powers to nominate subordinate officers. Jackson returns May 30 for Tennessee, leaving diplomats the headache of disentangling the international situation he created. His arrogance showing, Jackson reports to Calhoun that Florida is now American, and "I will assure you Cuba will be ours in a few days."

Jackson's Seminole War shocks the world into outrage, hastening threats of formal declaration of war from both England and Spain and shaking and frightening the Monroe administration. Fired-up Congress vows an investigation of the entire Jackson adventure.

But Washington officials, unlike the peppery Jackson, are divided and unsure. Congressional resolutions propose censure of the Indian fighter for his naked aggression. Yet Jackson's popularity, now meteoric, smothers any political advantage for punishing the nation's heroic border captain.

Popular with the people, Old Hickory's bold raid actually strengthens the Monroe administration's hand, leading to a virtual ultimatum for Madrid. Monroe defends Jackson's conduct, and informs Spain that it faces the alternatives of protecting and controlling the Floridas or ceding them to the United States.

In 1819, Spanish posts seized by Jackson in East Florida are returned to Spain, while Lt. Col. Jose Callava, the new governor, arrives in Pensacola with a garrison of troops and receives

Pensacola from the Americans. But already—as Callava finds the dilapidated town of 713 inhabitants largely in ruins—vigorous American instructions are leading the Madrid government to accede to U.S. demands.

Pensacola has hopes of structuring a municipality after the Constitution of 1812 is restored in 1820. Jose Noriega is elected first *alcalde,* but typically Callava refuses to recognize civil jurisdiction, aborting the experiment in self-government.

With the signing of the Adams-Onis or Transcontinental Treaty February 22, 1819, Spain renounces all claims to West Florida and cedes East Florida to the United States at a cost to the United States of $5 million in assumed claims against Spain. The western boundary of the United States is fixed at the Sabine, Red and Arkansas rivers and thence westward to the Pacific Ocean along the forty-second parallel. Spain retains Texas; the Americans gain most of the continent between Mexico and Canada.

With the final ratification of the treaty in 1821, Jackson returns to Pensacola for the last time—reluctantly the American provisional governor. Jackson's powerful will and military tenacity inspire the removal of troublesome international land-grabbers from the strategic Gulf Coast corner of the southeast. His action silences the persistent, bickering Spanish, and the Florida Cession opens Pensacola and the Floridas for American settlement.

Now Andrew Jackson's long shadow stretches across Plaza Ferdinand VII, for as Old Hickory intends, Pensacola, by the Eternal, *is* American.

And Governor Callava and *Alcalde* Noreiga wait for the American governor, neither clear as to limits of their fading authority.

Rachel Jackson was appalled by the wild spirit of Pensacola.
Pensacola Historical Society

Jackson's Route to Pensacola in 1821 from a map by Woodward Skinner
Andrew Jackson and Pensacola, *edited by James R. McGovern 1974.*

Pensacola in the 1850s.
Painting in the Historic Pensacola
Preservation Board Collection

5

An All American City

"The climate will suit you," President James Monroe tells pain-wracked Gen. Andrew Jackson, appointing him commissioner to receive possession of East and West Florida and as governor of the entire territory on March 12, 1821. Jackson doesn't want to return to Pensacola; his beloved, almost fanatically religious Rachel despises swampy, "heathenistic" Florida.

But he's finally persuaded. Jackson muses about his third and last visit; accept the provisional post for a short term, establish a territorial government on a firm basis, take care of my friends, complete the vindication of my Florida performance, and return home.

He retires his major general's stars, accepting the civil challenge in the further development of the southern coastal area, with the migration of people to help secure the frontier and "promote the welfare of the United States."

Among ten other officers assisting Jackson, Monroe appoints Col. James Grant Forbes marshal, sending him to Havana aboard the sloop USS *Hornet* to receive from the Cuban captain-general the necessary orders of His Majesty's authorities in Pensacola and St. Augustine for the surrender of Florida and its archives. The Spanish request American troops not enter Pensacola until Spanish forces are completely withdrawn, avoiding embarrassment and possible trouble be-

tween troops. The garrison will be transported to Cuba at American expense.

The Jacksons go by riverboat from Nashville to New Orleans, thence along the Gulf to Blakely, Alabama on Mobile Bay; then to Montpelier, Alabama, waiting five weeks at the army cantonment near the junction of Alabama and Tombigbee rivers for the Pensacola arrival of Forbes with transfer orders for Governor Jose Callava of West Florida.

Capt. Richard Keith Call, Tennessee lawyer serving as Jackson's aide-de-camp, interviews Callava, describing the Spanish governor as remarkably handsome—large, fair, blonde-haired, about forty, with regal bearing. But Call, optimistic, charmed by the dignified, exquisitely mannered Castilian and assessing him as a "frank, ingenuous soldier," cannot foresee the governor's reluctance and loyalist Spanish spirit.

As the weeks pass, the old Jacksonian impatience surfaces; he again imagines Spanish treachery. But this will be more Spanish procrastination. He begins correspondence with Callava, who knows his duty and absolutely refuses to initiate anything without written orders. They argue about protocol and ownership of cannon at Pensacola forts—both maneuvering, jockeying, venting stubborn pride.

But the impatient Jackson moves; he marches into Florida, stopping at Gonzalia, home of his old friend Don Manuel Gonzalez, fifteen miles north of Pensacola. It appears he plans storming the town by force. Instead he waits. Callava expects Jackson to make the first call. Equally proud, Jackson declares, "I will sink this place and him with it before I would visit him."

Finally, Jackson sidesteps protocol by ignoring it; he knows the cannon are his, after all, the big problem is Jackson doesn't speak Spanish and Callava knows no English. Yet, behaving badly, the Spanish invite Jackson' wrath.

Rachel Jackson, much fatigued by the verbal jousting, proceeds into Pensacola, occupying a house on Calle de Palafox at the corner of Calle de Intendencia owned by Dr. John Brosnaham. Governor Callava allows Dr. James C. Bronaugh, Jackson's personal physician and confidante, to prepare the residence for the American governor.

Arriving at the two-story house, Rachel, from the upstairs balcony, sees the broad blue bay three blocks south, beyond the weathered old Government House and the sandy Plaza; around her is the rustic old Spanish town with houses in ruins—alive with Spanish soldiers, seamen with knives in their belts, yellow women with well-turned limbs and insinuating glances, Jamaica blacks bearing prodigious burdens on their heads, fish peddlers hawking their catches from the bay, Seminoles hauntingly unfriendly, a grandee in his carriage, voices in Spanish and French, knots of ragtag Americans.

Rachel begs her husband to join her; he refuses, awaiting Callava's next gesture.

Forbes arrives in Pensacola June 9, but after more delay they finally agree on the date for the delivery of the Floridas: July 17, 1821.

Jackson predicts the wild, crowded American rush into the Floridas, and in a July 3 letter he writes, "I have no doubt but Pensacola will rise into notice as a commercial city faster than any other place in the United States."

At half past six on the morning of July 17, Jackson enters Pensacola, breakfasting with Rachel, Call, Bronaugh, Henry M. Brackenridge, and Forbes at the Governor's House. They are surrounded by the unpleasant airs of a boom town. Land speculators, swindlers, gamblers, soldiers of fortune—all swarming in, swelling the population to an estimated four thousand persons, three times the Spanish city's normal size.

Incessant rains combine with the heavy traffic to turn the sand streets to quagmires. "Heathen land," mutters Rachel, watching the languorous movement, seeing the vivid colors—the bay, the foliage, the houses "in ruins, old as time."

The Fourth Infantry band blares the arrival of Col. George M. Brooke and the American battalion, stepping briskly along Calle de Palafox, lining up across from Spanish dragoons of the Tarragona regiment in Plaza Ferdinand. The Stars and Stripes ride the hot, humid July morning air. The whole town seems agitated and in motion, excited about what is happening. The crowd bordering the Plaza is silent. Respectfully, the onlookers—many with tears in their eyes—make a lane for Jackson and his Americans. The largely Spanish population has only a vague notion of what life will be like under American rule, although under Gen. "Andres" Jackson the promise is frightening.

Old Hickory, brightly uniformed, stern of face, gallops his horse into the Plaza Ferdinand ceremonial scene between the saluting ranks for a ten o'clock appointment with Governor Callava. "Finally, the Americans are here," mutters Rachel, standing on a balcony overlooking the dusty plaza. She watches her husband move toward the old weathered Government House. At the steps, the agony of war and pain from old battle wounds and injuries from the dueling greens radiate from the general's pale countenance.

Earlier four companies of infantry under Maj. James E. Dinkins march to Fort San Carlos de Barrancas, exchanging flags. Seven days earlier, in St. Augustine, East Florida was formally transferred to Jackson's lieutenants.

Smiling, the tall, proud Callava greets Jackson. Snappy salutes break the humid air, and Jackson hands the Spaniard the instruments of his authority to take possession. Callava cites the May 5, 1821 mandate at Havana, surrendering West Florida. At the same time keys to the town, archives, and documents are surrendered; and Callava, as a final act, releases inhabitants of West Florida from their allegiance to Spain.

Slowly, solemnly, the Spanish royal banner is lowered to half mast. The American banner is raised slowly to the same point. Spanish soldiers salute, the red and gold flaring briefly, descending. And, with the Fourth Infantry band playing the *Star-Spangled Banner* for the first time in Pensacola and in Florida, the Stars and Stripes is hoisted one hundred feet into the air to the top of the flagstaff. In the bay, from the deck of the *Hornet,* a puff of smoke signals the first of twenty-one guns. Spanish Floridians, standing in the square, are choked with emotion—some cheer Jackson; some mantilla-cloaked Spanish women with big eyes mourn the loss of their homes and dread their lonely voyage to Havana.

The next day the Spanish garrison sails for Cuba, except for thirty-six officers allowed to stay, including former governor Callava.

Pensacola is American.

Already the old Spanish town reveals outward signs of Americanization. In the evening the Jacksons attend the performance of a traveling troupe in the hastily named Jacksonian Commonwealth Theatre, which enterprising manager Juan Baptiste Casenave converts from the rotunda dance hall next door to the story-and-a-half Tivoli House, a men's rendezvous on Calle de Zaragoza at Barracks Street.

Across the Plaza from the theater, E. Hathaway opens the Eagle Tavern, boasting hot and cold baths and "an elegant ten pin alley."

Jackson acts quickly. He creates Escambia County from West Florida lands east of the Perdido River and west of the Suwannee, and St. Johns County from the East Florida province, stretching the length of the peninsula. He creates three revenue districts—Pensacola, St. Marks, and St. Augustine—and civil government for the two counties. He wants all Indians removed from Creek territory, but begins setting up special reservations for all Florida Indians—numbering 3,899 in 1822— on the banks of the Apalachicola River adjoining the southern border of Alabama and Georgia and running down the river on both sides.

He appoints Brackenridge *alcalde,* a job held under the Spanish by Jose Noreiga, and names George Bowie Pensacola mayor. Within a week he organizes Pensacola's governing council with mayor and six alderman. He creates the offices of harbor master, constable, health officer, and resident physician. He appoints Call acting secretary of West Florida, awaiting the arrival of Monroe-appointed George Walton, and Dr. Bronaugh head of the Board of Health.

His ordinances—published in Spanish and English—call for "preservation of health," community protection, establishment of rates of pilotage, and registration of all inhabitants who wish to become American citizens.

In a sharp departure from Spanish rule, Jackson heeds the "blue law" desires of deeply religious Rachel, who bemoans "the Sabbath profanely kept." He cracks down on ungodly, unchristian, "demonic," and heathen activities.

Richard Keith Call.
Pensacola Historical Society

45

Within a week Rachel finds doors shut on the Sabbath, gambling houses demolished, fiddling and dancing, and cursing not heard on the Lord's Day. Ruling like a Christian soldier, Jackson prohibits public gaming houses and gambling except billiards, and forbids sale of liquor to soldiers.

Jackson, setting the government in motion, is bedeviled by land claims and patronage of speculators, job-seekers, and many cast-out Americans who think Pensacola will be a second New Orleans. He enjoys rewarding his friends, but the Monroe government ignores his recommendations and does not consult Jackson on appointments.

The new government finds little but decay—neglected, sun-washed shuttered houses of faded blue, green, and yellow surrounded by unkempt scrubs, weeping willows, Pearl of China, and sour orange trees. The Government House, propped up by unhewn timbers, appears unsafe; barracks built by the British have neither windows nor roofs, characterized by Jackson as "filthy" blockhouses. Nearby on Calle de Intendencia at the corner of Calle de Alcaniz stands the old British gaol (jail), now the Spanish calaboza. On the bayfront, only one nearly ruined pontoon wharf juts into the bay; most shipping is unloaded by lighters.

From the new print shop of Calle de Palafox, newspaper publishers Cary Nicholas and George Tunstall work around their newly arrived, hand-cranked flatbed press, transported by sea from Philadelphia. They prepare the first edition of *The Floridian,* August 18, 1821.

The four pages on the printer's stone for Pensacola's first newspaper is a sea of type, in English and Spanish: Jackson's proclamation concerning rights of territory residents and establishment of the American government; his letter to troops; death of Napoleon Bonaparte; lists of federal appointees; ode dedicated to Secretary of State John Quincy Adams; review focusing on an inaccurate description of Pensacola in a book by Col. James G. Forbes.

The editors extol a Jacksonian Commonwealth Theatre showing of *The Stranger* and a farce, *Fortune's Frolic,* with box seats one-dollar; praise the "Feats of Horsemanship" of Victor Pepin's equestrian circus; list the sale of Holland and American gin and Old Whiskey.

Nicholas and Tunstall are unaware that just four days earlier, in St. Augustine, the *Florida Gazette* had rolled off the press, jostling their prized first Pensacola newspaper from a choice position in history. Their publication is delayed by the slow delivery of the press, coupled with Governor Callava's refusal to allow the birth of the free press while Spanish colors are still flying. Actually *The Floridian* is the third newspaper founded in Florida—the first, St. Augustine's British Loyalist *East-Florida Gazette,* in 1763.

Nonetheless, a month after Jackson arrives, *The Floridian* symbolizes free institutions now on the West Florida horizon.

Even though Monroe's appointments frustrate Jackson, and the Spanish misread his outbursts, the volatile governor tries to accommodate Spanish inhabitants as tensions build between him and Callava. It finally explodes in a test of power with Monroe-appointed Eligius Fromentin, an ex-Jesuit priest expelled from France, now U.S. judge of West Florida.

The dignified Callava, Fromentin, and entrepreneur John Innerarity of the John Forbes and Company became close friends. And the break with Jackson comes over a question of the inheritance of Mercedes Vidal, a free quadroon and illegitimate daughter of the late Nicholas Maria Vidal, whose 1806 death leaves the Forbes company executor of an estate including large tracts of land in West Florida and Louisiana. The case remains unsettled for fifteen years, but Callava's friends persuade Fromentin to issue a writ of habeas corpus, even though the law had not been extended to the Floridas. Mercedes appeals to Brackenridge for assistance, and the *alcalde* takes the matter to Jackson.

In a provocative tug-of-war, Callava claims documents pertaining to the case are military papers not subject to transfer agreements. Angered, Jackson believes Callava is in collusion with the Forbes company to defraud the heirs. Jackson demands release of the papers. And Jackson's emissaries confront Callava, startling him at a dinner party with Fromentin, Innerarity, and the U.S. commander of troops. But the Castilian again stands his ground.

Later, Callava, accompanied by Innerarity, returns home, stricken with indigestion. But Jackson's troops follow. Finally Callava yields, demanding a written list of desired documents.

Jackson explodes, orders armed troops to Callava's house, and the Americans find the Spanish governor in bed, fully dressed except for his coat. Callava again refuses; the Americans demand he go before Governor Jackson. He surrenders his sword and accompanies the arresting party through the streets with a crowd following.

Callava confronts Jackson at ten o'clock at night, setting off a boiling, seething, screaming performance by both governors. "Surrender them!" Jackson bellows. But Callava bellows back.

His nerves shattered, Jackson tires of Callava's resistance, explodes, pounds the table, frightens onlookers, and remands Col. Jose Callava to prison. Callava's carted off to the small, dirty, uncomfortable British-built gaol.

Entering the jail, accompanied by a large contingent of Spanish officers, Callava humorously sees the insanity of it all. He rears back, roaring with laughter. Soon chairs, cots and beds are brought in, along with food, cigars, claret, and champagne. Joking, they make a night of it, imitating "Don Andrew Jackson, Governor of Florida."

But Jackson, proving supreme, orders the papers in question removed from Callava's residence and summons Judge Fromentin before him. Jackson unleashes a tongue-lashing that settles the question of his extensive judicial powers over the territory. He then quickly rules on the inheritance, predictably favoring the heirs.

Callava leaves jail the next day, bemoaning his treatment, and rushes to Washington in protest. But Secretary of State John Quincy Adams rationalizes Jackson's actions as valid.

While Callava snorts and fumes in Washington, Spanish officers in Pensacola take one last jab at the irascible Jackson. They publish their protest, aiming to incite the public against Jackson and continue the uproar in Washington over the administration of Florida.

But Jackson, now convinced he must leave Florida for the Hermitage soon, gives the entire staff of Spanish officers four days to get out of the country. They hurriedly depart, but not before composing a final blast at the American they believe is a lunatic governor who might easily initiate a war with Spain to satisfy his craving for power.

But Jackson holds firm; later, expressing gratitude to Jackson for acquiring the Floridas, his Washington allies blunt all attempts to vote Congressional censure.

On the night of October 3 Andrew and Rachel Jackson attend a farewell party in Austin's Tavern on Calle de Palafox. Military officers and Pensacola citizens hear the American governor say, "I have made no discrimination of persons. Say what you will, Andrew Jackson treated everyone equally. My house has

Don Manuel Gonzalez house at Gull Point on Escambia Bay.
Pensacola Historical Society

been surrounded by no guards, and no one has been kept at a distance by repulsive formalities; all have had free admittance and found a ready ear, when they required my aid for the protection of their rights . . . the American government is the freest and strongest in the world."

Amid toasts of honor and applause, Jackson ends his slightly more than eleven weeks as Florida governor—a job he'd not wanted and hated. He now knows if he doesn't quit a thankless job and return to Tennessee before winter, he might be carried home in a pine box.

But he knows Pensacola harbor will be strategically important for coastal defense; he sees two virtually different Spanish Floridas emerging as a new state rather than being annexed to others. And one of the evening's toasts hints of the long West Florida debate than unforeseen; "The state of Alabama—we love her as a sister, but would not be wed."

Three days later the Jacksons depart Government House in a carriage drawn by four gray horses. He leaves behind a well-organized government and friends Brackenridge, Call and James Gadsden.

George Walton, Jr., son of Dorothy Walton and his Georgian father who had signed the Declaration of Independence, becomes acting governor in the governmental transition continuing in the family legacy. William Duval, inheriting the Jacksonian legacy, will become the first official territorial governor when the Floridas become an official territory of the United States on March 30, 1822.

Jackson is back in Nashville in November, knowing no other foreign powers will threaten Pensacola. George Walton, Jr., forecasts the general's future in a prophetic December 10, 1821 letter: "Let it be Known that you are a Candidate for the Presidency of the United States, and the descendants of those men, who, by their acts, emancipated us from the yoke of George Third, will rally around you."

Walton's revolutionary spirit manifests in his Georgian mother, daughter of British Loyalist Tom Camber who had married American Loyalist and Georgia Congressman George Walton in 1778. Dorothy Walton lives in a cottage at 211 East Romana Street until her death. Buried in St. Michael's Cemetery, Dorothy Walton is revered as Pensacola matriarch of the Jacksonian period. Her legacy remains in the apron-roofed, porched wooden cottage, rescued and preserved by historian T. T. Wentworth, Jr., for his historical museum on its original East Romana Street site and then relocated on Zaragoza Street in 1968 as a landmark interpretative house within the Seville Square Historical District. After her death, George Walton, Jr., becomes a Mobile attorney and mayor of the Alabama city.

Now a titanic force of freedom will make Florida the twenty-seventh star in the American flag. The Florida liberator becomes President Jackson, the seventh American president, elected to the first of two terms in 1828.

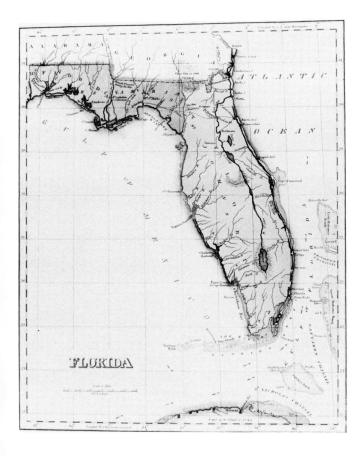

Map of Florida showing the two original counties, Escambia and St. Johns, carved from Spanish West and East Florida.
Pensacola Historical Society

Henry Marie Brackenridge.
Pensacola Historical Society

A sketch of Warrington in the 1850s.
Pensacola Historical Society

P A R T

6

Navy Town In Isolation

Even before Jackson's governorship, Americans envision Pensacola Bay as a location for a naval depot and coastal defenses. Now Jackson's successors know they need more—roads, commerce, governmental assistance, links with the outside world. The old Spanish settlement on the edge of a commodious bay lacks major waterways draining the fertile back country.

Envisioning Pensacola as an emporium of Southern trade and commerce, town builders face a roadless wilderness, looking to waterways, fretting for lack of navigable streams beyond the sprawling bay.

Led by Territorial Governor Duval, Virginian and former East Florida federal judge, Pensacolians press for a navy yard, roads and transportation canals during the Legislative Council's first assembly in the temporary capital on June 10, 1822.

Duval is joined by George Walton as secretary of Florida, and Henry M. Brackenridge presides over the federal court at Pensacola. Already throngs of adventurers, opportunists, and office-seekers present for the American transfer find little to feed their dreams and drift away, rapidly reducing Pensacola's population as its governors begin seeking ways to turn the harbor and surrounding wilderness into commercial profit.

But already geography—specially Pensacola's isolation—portends the shape of Florida's future and the Gulf Coast city's brief time as the seat of territorial government. With no roads in the wilderness, St. Augustine delegates encounter long travel difficulties, and a quorum is not present until July 22. Dr. Bronaugh, resident physician of the Board of Health, presides, but finds himself battling another Jackson colleague, Richard Keith Call, for selection as congressional delegate.

Yet the ambitious Pensacolians face a more severe enemy—"yellow jack." The epidemic of August 10-17 sends legislators into session north of the city at the Gull Point home of Don Juan de la Rua, and later to the ranch of Don Manuel Gonzalez. But they cannot escape: Dr. Bronaugh dies, and out of the chaotic deliberations the Legislative Council selects Joseph M. Hernandez of St. Augustine delegate to Congress.

Ravages of the yellow fever epidemic reduce Pensacola's population from 1,500 to 1,000, wiping out many of the Americans. By September's Council adjournment, Governor Duval faces a catastrophe that alarms Jackson, who laments Dr. Bronaugh's death and charges it all to Pensacola's uncleanliness.

Already dreams of a navy yard are galvanizing the Pensacolians, but the legislators tackle a first priority—roads, including the Pensacola-St. Augustine artery that will eliminate the tortuous

One of the earliest photographic aerials of Pensacola as seen from Palafox Hill appears to have been taken from the roof of the Edward A. Perry House at Wright and Palafox streets, circa 1860-1870.
Pensacola Historical Society

Commodore Lewis Warrington, 1826, first Navy Yard commandant.
U.S. Navy

Capt. Melanchton T. Woolsey.
U.S. Navy

overland journey of seven hundred miles through Georgia and Alabama. The laborious journeying through Florida wilds come into focus when Congress declines to designate either Pensacola or St. Augustine as territorial capital, fixing Pensacola as location for the first Legislative Council and St. Augustine for the second 1823 session.

Travel-weary legislators propose a trans-Florida highway between the two cities, a project Congress approves in 1824. The narrow, stump-dotted highway runs from Deer Point on the Santa Rosa peninsula (Gulf Breeze) along the old Indian trail to Cow Ford on the Choctawhatchee River (Point Washington), east to the Chipola River, then through redlands to Ocheesee Bluff on the Apalachicola, and east to Fort San Luis of Apalachee and along the old Spanish trail to St. Augustine.

Woefully inadequate, and years in the making, the road stirs complaints; tree stumps in the roadbed were left so high wagons and stagecoaches cannot pass over them.

In 1824 wearied legislators agree on a new capital at midpoint along the old Spanish trail crossing the Tallahassee hills. The capitol is born in a log cabin for the third Legislative Council, and legislators retain the Indian name Tallahassee, meaning "old town" and also translated as "old field." Now Pensacolians look east of the Apalachicola River for the seat of government; Governor Duval and territorial officials relocate to Tallahassee, feeding rivalry between East and West Florida.

Pensacola turns to internal improvements, chief among them inadequate roads linking with Alabama. A carriage road connects with a Perdido River ferry, linking Pensacola with Blakely, Alabama. And a seven-mile shoreline trail from Pensacola to Barrancas requires crossing two bayous, possible by horseback at low tide.

Unlike other Gulf ports—Apalachicola, Mobile, New Orleans—Pensacola lacks navigable rivers draining the extensive interior for developing its harbor. And visionaries infected with "canal fever" propose water connections with Mobile Bay, New Orleans, the Apalachicola River; even the Atlantic Ocean by a cross-peninsula canal. But canal talk is empty speculative rhetoric, no shovels turn, and by the mid-1830s Pensacolians look to a steam railway for passage of cotton and other exports to markets along the Atlantic.

The Pensacola Legislative Council gives shape

to Pensacola's future in its congressional petition for harbor fortifications and a naval station, citing the harbor as the superior Gulf location. By 1825, President John Quincy Adams signs a congressional bill authorizing a Gulf navy yard in territorial Florida.

Tampa Bay is Pensacola's only competitor. Site-selection commissioners Lewis Warrington, William Bainbridge, and James Biddle survey the west shore of the Pensacola bay from Fort San Carlos de Barrancas to British-named Tartar Point and Deer Point. And they also survey Town Point and English and Spanish coves of the east shore; they choose Pensacola. By the end of 1826 Congress authorizes plans and funds for the Pensacola Lighthouse and the Tartar Point installation under supervision of Commodore Warrington, first Navy Yard commandant. Warrington's successor, Commandant Melanchon T. Woolsey, creates two villages—Warrington and Woolsey—immediately outside the Yard where workers lease lots for home building.

Despite meager funds from Washington snail's pace construction in the prosperous 1830s, the Tartar Point base takes shape along sandy shores amid oak and pine. There are elegant, symmetric brick and white buildings—officers' quarters, workshops, warehouses, hospital with ionic columns, lighthouse, and a wharf and docking facilities. Already vessels cruising the West Indies turn to Pensacola as a supply base rather than Thompson's Island (Key West).

Jackson's vision for Pensacola included major harbor defenses, and by 1829 Congress appropriates more than $100,000 for protective fortifications. Arsenals in Augusta, Georgia, and Baton Rouge, Louisiana, are too distant to supply the southern frontier with arms and munitions of war; fortifications surrounding the Pensacola yard—on sites originally chosen by Spain and Great Britain—make the coastal area impregnable against outside attack.

The task goes to Capt. William Henry Chase of the Army Corps of Engineers, an 1815 West Point graduate, bringing a decade of engineering and construction experience from New York to New Orleans to his job as chief engineer for the area of the Gulf of Mexico. Supervising defenses from Louisiana to Key West, Chase arrives in Pensacola in 1826 as a fort builder, yet proves an imaginative businessman and entrepreneur, promoting Pensacola's brick manufacturing industry while constructing the network of harbor

Maj. William Henry Chase.
Pensacola Historical Society

Restored Fort Barrancas, one of the forts built as part of the Pensacola Harbor defense plan, sits behind restored Spanish water Battery San Antonio (sometimes called "Fort San Carlos"). Administered by the National Park Service, both are located within the Naval Air Station.
Pensacola Historical Society

fortifications to protect the Navy Yard.

Chase builds Fort Pickens (1834) on the western (Siquenza) point of Santa Rosa Island, and Fort McRee (1839) on Foster's Bank (Perdido Key) to flank the harbor entrance, and Fort Barrancas (1844) on the high bluff (La Barranca or Red Cliffs, site of Fort San Carlos de Austria) facing the entrance. Army engineers revamp Battery San Antonio (built in 1797), and begin the Advanced Barrancas Redoubt in 1859 midway between the bluff and Bayou Grande to defend the Navy Yard from land attack.

Meanwhile, Navy Secretary Samuel L. Southard, seeking timber resources for building and repairing ships, formulates the nation's first comprehensive naval live oak reservation program with purchase of the 1,337.87-acre Deer Point tract for $4,900 in 1828. Southard envisions a 60,000-acre system of naval live oaks reservations surrounding the Pensacola yard.

With the Deep South's symbolic live oak envisioned as the prized durable timbers for shipbuilding, President Adams establishes the Deer Point Naval Live Oak Plantation on the Santa Rosa peninsula as the young nation's first experimental tree farm and only naval live oak plantation project ever established by the United States. Judge Henry M. Brackenridge owns 1,360 acres in the center of government land on the peninsula, sells 340 acres to the U.S. Navy for $2,200, and becomes the first Naval Live Oaks superintendent. The plantation system—expanded to approximately 150,000 acres, 90,000 in the Florida Territory—continues until the outbreak of the Civil War when shipbuilders develop ironclads. Today most of the original wilderness preserve east of Gulf Breeze stands symbolic of America's first forest conservation program as a recreation park and headquarters for Gulf Islands National Seashore.

With Naval officers enlivening Pensacola society, participating in Fourth of July and George Washington Birthday celebrations, and Captain Chase and his Army officers supervising work on harbor forts with contracted slave labor, Pensacolians begin a promising relationship with its military community. Pensacolians fraternize with crews from U.S. and French squadrons summering in the harbor; Pensacola daughters marry Navy men; and, on a larger scale, the Pensacola-U.S. Navy marriage becomes one of economics, politics, and social graces. By 1833, the first financial institution—Bank of Pensacola, organized with the vision of Captain Chase and

merchants two years earlier—reflects increasing military expenditures, rising timber economy, and dreams of a railroad north.

The Floridian, which in 1821 commented "nature has done more for this city than any other on this continent," falters and fails as the city's first newspaper; In 1824, W. Hasell Hunt launches the *Pensacola Gazette* and *West Florida Advertiser,* an independent voice espousing Republican principles, forerunner of the dominant *Pensacola Gazette,* edited by Pennsylvania lawyer Benjamin Drake Wright from 1834 to 1845. Wright, arriving in 1823, emerges among the ablest and most influential territorial journalists, championing Pensacola economic development as spokesman for conservative Whigs. Wright begins his meteoric rise to Pensacola mayor and appointment as chief justice of the first state Supreme Court of Florida in 1853.

He is a member of the Legislative Council and U.S. attorney for West Florida in 1824. By the 1830s his *Gazette* strongly advocates an inland waterway between New Orleans and Pensacola and shares Captain Chase's dream of a railroad to Columbus, Georgia.

Chase gains Bank of Pensacola financial backing for trackage north to Georgia and Alabama and a "New Town" east of Pensacola along the proposed rail route. Among the most ambitious of numerous territorial railroad projects, the Pensacola-inspired Florida, Alabama & Georgia Railroad Company projects 210 miles of track connecting the Gulf seaport with Columbus, Georgia's Chattahoochee River cotton-commerce town. Pensacola's first proposed rail penetration into the interior includes a branch line to Montgomery, Alabama, giving the Florida harbor access to cotton plantations of the Alabama-Georgia heartland.

The Columbus connection is doomed, mired in sectional politics, from the outset. Mobilians—protective of shipping interests on navigable waterways into the Alabama interior; fearing Pensacola's competition—successfully block legislative efforts for the Montgomery road. Still, Alabama planters—disappointed by dependence on rivers frequently running low during the shipping season—voice strong support.

Chase and backers win approval from the Territorial Council, and gain a $2.5 million stock issue from the Bank of Pensacola. Congress authorizes an engineering survey, sixty-foot right-of-way through public lands and timbering privileges within one hundred yards of the roadbed. But Washington rejects their request for 600,000 acres of federally owned land.

Engineers map a route running eastward out of Pensacola through the Escambia swamp, over the mouth of the Escambia River and northward to the Alabama-Florida boundary in the vicinity of present-day Jay, Florida, leading into the Conecuh River valley. The Alabama route follows the Conecuh River northeast to Columbus.

Imported Irish and Dutch workmen—often fighting, pausing for steins of beer—chop through swampy bogs, grading the roadbed and building trestles.

In 1837, the Alabama legislature reverses itself by allowing the route to the Alabama capital; the Pensacola railroad company compromises, reducing trackage to the 156-mile Montgomery route. But beleaguered directors, with ten miles of grade and trestle virtually complete to the river and six miles east of the river—are further diminished by the 1837 national financial panic reducing the Bank of Pensacola to shambles. The bank seizes company assets; rails and rolling stock remain unused on Pensacola docks.

With prosperity returning in the 1840s—and Alabama annexation and statehood talk arousing the speculative urge of Pensacola visionaries—Chase and investors return with a newly chartered Alabama & Florida Railroad Company, projecting a new, northerly Montgomery route. Surveyors, avoiding the treacherous swamp and river-crossing, map the road from its bayfront wharf and depot site on Tarragona Street north and west of the Escambia River forty-five miles to join Alabama rails being laid by a companion Alabama company led by Charles T. Pollard from Montgomery to an Alabama point just north of the state boundary which they name Pollard Station.

Congress in 1856 grants alternate sections of land lying along the railroad route to states of Alabama and Florida. Chase, continuing his railroading affiliation while supervising fort construction, resigns from the U.S. Army with the rank of major in 1856, ending a thirty-seven year career, and accepts the presidency of the Alabama & Florida Railroad.

The *Pensacola Gazette* reflects townspeople's enthusiasm as the Pensacola-Montgomery rails are joined: "Joy to Pensacola! Clear the Track! The Railroad is Coming. The engineer has arrived . . ." Displaying bravado, foreseeing thousands of bales of cotton and tons of produce for Pensacola shipment to Europe and the North,

Jackson Morton, brickmaker and Navy agent, served in the U.S. Senate in the 1850s.
Pensacola Historical Society

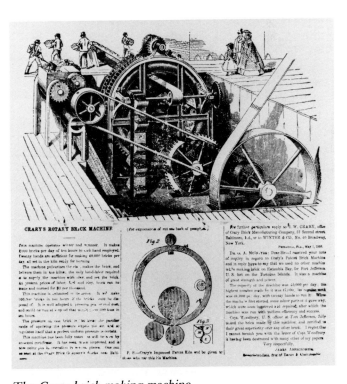

The Crary brick-making machine produced millions of bricks for the federal government in the 1850s. John W. Crary, the inventor, came to Pensacola in the 1850s to establish the Abercrombie brickyard.
Pensacola Historical Society

the *Gazette* editor warns Pensacola's competitors: "It will in a few years be necessary for people of New Orleans to send to us for the necessaries of life and Mobile will be desolate only for us."

Rails thread through timber country where settlers harvest long-leaf yellow pine for Pensacola mills. "Square" timber, hewn from logs in four cuts, are tied together as rafts and floated down the Escambia River to Ferry Pass, just north of Pensacola. Crews following the river as much as one hundred miles then travel by rail to Pollard and logging camps dotting the stream-veined interior. A stagecoach follows the old Indian trading thoroughfare, Wolf Path, but with the new railroad passengers travel south from Pollard to stations at Bluff Springs, Milner's, Pine Barren, Cooper's Station, Bayard's, Gonzales, Oakfield, and Pensacola. Passengers can travel from Montgomery to Pensacola in about ten hours.

Faced with shortages of labor, Chase and Navy commandants turn to slave contractors such as Jasper Strong and Byrd Willis and the years-long military construction expands slavery. Skillful black masons weave an architectural artistry as million of bricks go into Pensacola's forts. And kiln owners—among them, H. I. Ingraham, Bacon and Abercrombie, Jackson Morton—then export brick, principally to New Orleans, especially for construction of Fort Jefferson on the Dry Tortugas. Morton, beginning as a small Blackwater River brickmaker, becomes Navy agent and finally, by the 1850s, a conservative Whig U.S. Senator.

Despite other endeavors—tanning, shipbuilding, iron casting, a cotton mill—Pensacolians turn to the rich pine forests, expanding the colonial harvesting industry that had provided shipmasts, firewood, and naval stores.

By the early 1830s, with Joseph M. White luring New York and Maine investors and lumbermen to Pensacola, more than two dozen mills expand small-scale pineywoods operations along the Perdido, Escambia, and Blackwater rivers. Among timber pioneers, South Carolinian Joseph Forsyth purchases Juan de la Rua's Pond Creek land tract on the eastern shore of Escambia Bay in 1828. He erects a dam for water power for sawing lumber and joins with Andrew and Ezekiel Simpson to develop the extensive Forsyth-Simpson manufacturing company at the sawmill town he calls Arcadia, at the mouth of the creek leading to the Blackwater River. He develops the three-mile, mule-powered Arcadia railroad to the Blackwater River—first for the Pensacola Bay area. Anticipating a boom for his pineywoods holdings, Forsyth moves his growing operations to a new mill site and community near the Blackwater River, named Bagdad, and transforms his original Arcadia site into a steam-powered cotton mill that by 1853 is Florida's largest cotton factory, producing more than 600,000 yards of cloth annually.

The Forsyth-Simpson Bagdad sawmill sets the pace for West Florida lumbering. By 1860, the company has a capital investment of $175,000, employs 150 people with slaves doing much of the labor, and annually saws 40,000 logs. Only three other companies—Crigler, Batchelder and Company, Mir and McVoy, and E. A. Pearce and Son—rival Forsyth and Simpson among eighteen mills employing 600 people and producing almost 55 million feet of lumber exported from Pensacola wharves to markets throughout the world.

As the 1830s and 1840s evolve, a few private schools open, providing meager training for young men only. Yet a rising religious fervor permeates Pensacola; religious pioneers organize congregations and build churches. The Catholic church creates the Florida and Alabama diocese in 1829; by 1833 the St. Michael's Parish completes its first church, replacing the old converted British warehouse. The bishop in Mobile authorizes Warrington's St. John the Evangelist parish in 1851.

The first Episcopal Christ Church facing Seville Square, designed in the Christopher Wren tradition and completed in 1832, symbolizes rise of the Protestant faith. Old Christ Church becomes one of the city's enduring landmarks as Methodists, Presbyterians, and Baptists reshape the old Spanish settlement with new edifices.

Today Old Christ Church, Florida's oldest still-standing protestant church building, is the Pensacola Historical Museum, home of Pensacola Historical Society. It continues its long heritage after Episcopalians move to the new Christ Church at the corner of Wright and Palafox streets in 1903. Used by parishioners of Saint Cyprian's Episcopal Church, Old Christ Church houses the city library from the 1930s to the late 1950s when the first municipal library building opens at the corner of Gregory and Spring streets; by 1960 it's the city's popular hometown museum and landmark, symbolic of the historical preservation movement transforming the Seville Square neighborhood in the early 1960s.

Naturally, victims of geographical isolation, West Floridians jealously protect sectional interests as population and political power of Middle Florida—spawned by the Tallahassee capital—and East Florida grow rapidly. Pensacola loses its vigorous champion in Washington when Joseph M. White replaces Richard Keith Call in 1825 and the congressional seat passes to East Florida's Charles Downing in 1837 and David Levy in 1841.

New territorial counties—Santa Rosa east of the Escambia River in 1842—begin West Florida's political subdivision aimed at counterbalancing those east of the Apalachicola River. Pensacolians' declining voice in Florida affairs intensify feelings that West Florida's future—due to geography—is annexation to Alabama. Arguments focus on protection from the Alabama militia, greater ease of more centrally locating the Florida capital and West Florida's colonial independence from East Florida under Britain and Spain.

As early as 1822, Alabama Senator John Williams leads an unsuccessful legislative campaign for West Florida annexation. By the 1840s, with statehood being debated, Alabama annexation arguments fill pages of the *Pensacola Gazette,* territorial legislators petition the U.S. Senate in opposition to separation, and Pensacolians rally at a public meeting, requesting West Florida union with Alabama. In 1844, the territorial legislature reverses itself, asking separation, presumably so the region west of the Apalachicola River might join Alabama.

Pensacola sentiment for joining Alabama goes hand and hand with opposition to statehood; few support admission to the union until the 1838-39 St. Joseph Constitutional Convention to draft basic law for the proposed state of Florida. Escambia delegates, led by Benjamin Wright, Jackson Morton, and Thomas M. Blount, intend to support East Florida, stalling statehood discussions. But the Escambians are stymied by East Floridians who surprisingly favor proceeding, and the written constitution diminishes the old argument for Alabama annexation.

On July 4, 1845, less than a month after the death of President Andrew Jackson, Pensacola is the westernmost town of the twenty-seventh state in the American union. Still basically a military harbor, Pensacola becomes the dream of shipbuilders and timber exporters—ambitions soon

Mr. and Mrs. Ezekiel Ewing Simpson. Mr. Simpson helped pioneer West Florida industry with the manufacturing and lumber firm of Forsyth and Simpson at Arcadia and Bagdad. Pensacola Historical Society

shadowed by festering national internal strife centering on the slavery question.

Despite dreaded yellow fever—epidemics taking toll of the fluctuating population in the 1850s—Pensacola grows as rails join at Pollard in 1857 and Pensacola Bay area sawmills produce 54,913,000 feet of sawed lumber by the end of the decade. Stephen Russell Mallory, Trinidad-born, Key-West-raised Pensacola lawyer who married Angela Moreno, eldest daughter of Don Francisco Moreno, goes to the U.S. Senate in 1850 and proves himself a naval innovator, promoting shipbuilding, including two vessels built at the Pensacola Navy Yard between 1857 and 1859, USS *Seminole* and USS *Pensacola.*

Ironically, Mallory in Washington helps build the federal Navy under darkening clouds drawing him and other Floridians into the simmering North-South argument that eventually brings war to the harbor of his adopted hometown.

Pensacola's first brush with the impending crisis is the notoriety of anti-slavery martyr Jonathan Walker, an outspoken Massachusetts abolitionist whose treatment of Pensacola blacks as equals and friends offends his Pensacola neighbors. Leaving Pensacola for the British Bahamas with seven black slaves in 1844, Walker and the fugitives are apprehended near the Florida Keys. Returned to Pensacola and charged with stealing slaves, Walker is saved by the sheriff and deputies from lynching by holding an angry mob at bay with pistols. Abolitionist newspapers described Walker's imprisonment and trial. Serving time on the pillory, he's pelted by rotten eggs. Worse, he's branded on the hand—SS for slave stealer. John Greenleaf Whittier immortalizes the Pensacola incident in the popular poem "The Branded Hand."

Meanwhile, oldtime Whigs opposing statehood and following *Gazette* demands that Jackson Morton serve as West Florida's U.S. senator decline in popularity; the issue of slavery and states rights gradually erode their power. Yet, West Floridians still resent political dominance of other regions of Florida. They successfully pass 1856 legislation authorizing a referendum on the annexation question. Governor James E. Broome's veto of the legislation angers Pensacolians; the *Gazette* reports "annexation favored by a large majority of the people."

By 1860, with war talk filling Pensacola streets, most Pensacolians support the Democrats, who now favor another form of separation—secession of Southern states.

Still, on the eve of Civil War, Gregory Street is practically Pensacola's northern boundary. Palafox Street from Garden Street north is a wagon road crowded by dense titi swamps except at Chase Street. Captain Chase's New Town resembles a blackjack waste, modified only by the broken outline of the first railroad cut slicing through the woods toward Carpenter's Creek.

Even though U.S. war vessels are often at the Navy Yard, the Palafox Street wharf is the only practicable landing for sailing vessels. On moonlit nights, young gentlemen and ladies promenade along the unbroken expanse of the bay, seeing the shadowy outline of soldierless Fort Pickens on the pine-pocked sand barrier jutting into the harbor. And many Pensacolians speaking Spanish as universally as English and familiar with French turn conversations to the fate of their sleepy harbor town as Southern emotions fever the inevitability of secession.

Old Christ Church, built in 1832, is now the home of the Pensacola Historical Museum, established in 1960. Pensacola Historical Society

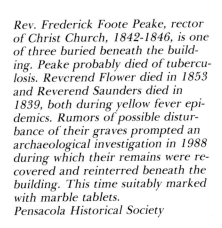

Rev. Frederick Foote Peake, rector of Christ Church, 1842-1846, is one of three buried beneath the building. Peake probably died of tuberculosis. Reverend Flower died in 1853 and Reverend Saunders died in 1839, both during yellow fever epidemics. Rumors of possible disturbance of their graves prompted an archaeological investigation in 1988 during which their remains were recovered and reinterred beneath the building. This time suitably marked with marble tablets. Pensacola Historical Society

Dr. Eugenio Antonio Sierra was chief medic for the royal Spanish hospital. His family remained and prospered under the Americans.
Pensacola Historical Society

United States Marshal Ebenezer Dorr brands the hand of Jonathan Walker "SS" for slave stealer. His story is told in his memoirs, Trial and Imprisonment of Jonathan Walker at Pensacola, Florida For Aiding Slaves to Escape from Bondage.
Pensacola Historical Society

Clara Louise Garnier, a native of France, married George Barkley. Their marriage, which produced seven children, has been called a marriage of cultures. Their house still stands as one of the city's preserved landmarks.
Pensacola Historical Society

The Barkley House on Florida Blanca
Street has a blending of French and
Spanish styles typical of the Gulf Coast
region. It has been restored as the official residence of Pensacola operated
by the Pensacola Heritage Foundation.
Pensacola Historical Society

Don Francisco Moreno, often referred
to as the "Father of Pensacola," produced twenty-seven children and numerous grandchildren.
Pensacola Historical Society

WILSON'S ZOUAVES IN THE DITCH AND COVERED WAY ON THE LAND FRONT OF FORT PICKENS.—SKETCHED BY AN OFFICER OF THE FORT.—[SEE PAGE 471.]

This drawing of Fort Pickens, by an officer of the fort, shows Wilson's Zouaves in the ditches on March 6, 1861. Harper's Weekly print, July 27, 1861. Pensacola Historical Society

7

Rehearsal for the Firestorm

In the sun-washed harbor, on shifting sands, Fort Pickens stands a lonely vigil. The sprawling, pentagonal brick sentinel, a mosaic of mortared-brick arches connecting massive walls pocked with wide, yawning gunports, looms ominously against the wintry January sky as Floridians move toward secession.

Sea breezes buffet the walls, hurrying sheets of tiny white quartz crystals across the empty parade ground and into the long, dark and dank corridors.

Inside the fortress, moisture seeps from the bricked ceilings and drips in pools. Walls of the mortared chambers groan, settling into a rigidity, resisting forces of nature and ravages of time.

With war clouds floating south, cannonless, soldierless Fort Pickens is now more an unused, eroding tool of harbor defense than it appears from the Pensacola mainland and in faraway Washington. The Fort is more neglect than strength of coastal cannon defense, one of three Pensacola guardians of the Gulf against the possibility of an invading armada that, so far, has not arrived.

Built by William Chase thirty years earlier, and last fitted for war when guns sounded on bloody Mexican fields, Fort Pickens stands in muted desolation.

Across the South, in the new year of 1861, secessionist emotions ride the shoulders of Southern pride; cotton states' politicians hammer out a new and uncertain republic they call the Confederate States of America, forging a second American Revolution. In Washington, D.C., a lean, gaunt, rail-splitting lawyer from Illinois, Abraham Lincoln, arrives at his White House presidential desk for his first of many crises destined to haunt the newly elected first Republican chief executive of the United States of America.

Unknown to newly elected President Lincoln, faraway Fort Pickens is already a symbol of Southern resistance. Another, in Charleston harbor, is Fort Sumter. Pensacola or Charleston. Pickens or Sumter. The question: where will war, if it must come, begin?

Seeds of secession sprout across Florida after the 1860 Black Republican victory. Extremists vent anger; moderates like former territorial governor Richard Keith Call, cautioning against treason and "opening the gates of Hell, from which shall flow the curses of the damned to sink you to perdition," are lost in the stampede. On January 10, with A. W. Nicholson and S. H. Wright of Escambia County and Jackson Morton and E. E. Simpson of neighboring Santa Rosa County representing the basically anti-secessionist view of West Floridians, the Secession Convention in Tallahassee votes to take Florida out of the union the day after Mississippi proclaims its independence and only a few hours before Alabama votes to follow the path of South Carolina.

Now living in a "sovereign and independent nation," Pensacolians raise money for military supplies and support families of men joining volunteer companies. Massachusetts-born and Yale educated lawyer Edward Aylesworth Perry, destined to rise to Confederate brigadier general, captains the Pensacola Rifle Rangers; and Capt. Alexander Bright commands the Pensacola Guards. Florida Governor Madison S. Perry appoints retired U.S. Army Col. William H. Chase to organize the state militia and occupy Pensacola fortifications.

Pensacola, remote from Fort Sumter, where war came like a fire bell in the night, contribute the first-act episode in the four-year Civil War. And Pensacola's sudden emergence with Charleston as pawns on President Lincoln's chessboard in 1861 catapults the Gulf Coast harbor into national eminence, if only briefly.

With war inevitable, stakes are high in Pensacola. The city's location on the best natural harbor on the Gulf Coast, her naval and civilian shipyards, and a nearly completed railroad to Montgomery, Alabama, make the West Florida military city a valuable prize for the emerging Confederacy.

Pensacola's active Navy Yard consists of a million-dollar drydock, workshops, warehouses, barracks, a marine hospital, and cannons and ammunition valued at half a million dollars.

Naturally with U.S. troops already in Pensacola harbor, the old Spanish town is important to Washington. Federal occupation of Santa Rosa Island, which defended the mouth of Pensacola harbor, will nullify advantages to Southerners, who in the opening days of 1861 gather in Pensacola to defend the coast and train for war.

Florida secessionists, aroused by Washington's strategy to reinforce the Pensacola forts and destroy the Federal Arsenal at Chattahoochee, react quickly: Quincy Guards seize the Apalachicola River ammunition supply base, the coup netting a gold mine of small arms; and a handful of volunteers grab the lone Federal sentry guarding Fort Marion at St. Augustine; others seize Fort Clinch at Fernandina.

Then, nervous Floridians and Alabamians focus on Pensacola. Alabama Governor A. B. Moore dispatches state troops to seize Forts Morgan and Gaines at the mouth of Mobile Bay, and heeds Governor Perry's urgent request, rushing five companies to Pensacola.

Carrying an American flag with a lone star, the Alabamians join Colonel Chase's gathering Florida troops ordered to take possession of Federal property.

On January 5, 1861—the day after Alabamians seize the Mobile Bay forts—Florida Senator David L. Yulee in Washington says "the immediate important thing to be done is occupation of the forts. The Naval Station and Pensacola forts are of first consequence."

Pensacola's fortifications are not garrisoned. Maj. John Winder, then absent on leave; ironically destined to become a Confederate brigadier general connected with Southern military prisons, commands fifty-one men of Company G, First U.S. Artillery, at Barrancas Barracks. But now the Army command falls to First Lt. Adam J. Slemmer. Commodore James Armstrong has thirty-eight Marines and eighty ordinary seamen in his Navy Yard command, along with the steamer *Wyandotte* with a crew of seventy-eight, and the storeship *Supply* with thirty-six men.

Now—in the tense harbor—the stage was set for the months-long Fort Pickens-or-Fort Sumter confrontation beginning the night of January 8, 1861, on the drawbridge at Fort Barrancas.

It's six hours before cadets of the Citadel fire on the Union supplyship *Star of the West* entering Charleston harbor; two weeks before Jefferson Davis rises in the U.S. Senate to say farewell; and three months before Gen. Pierre Beauregard's Southern cannon belch flame over Fort Sumter and ignite the American War Between the States.

Slemmer, acting cautiously to the arrival of Florida and Alabama troops in Pensacola, posts guards to protect the ammunition stores.

Near midnight, Slemmer's Federal guards, watching shadows as moonlight plays over Pensacola's harbor, discover movement in the stillness. Lurking figures near the Barrancas drawbridge: Secessionists! Quickly, now, the sharp challenge:

"Halt! Who goes there?"

Silence.

Sentries find the triggers of their muskets. *Crack! Crack! Crack!*

The drum rolls. Inside the barracks, feet hit the floor. Leaping from their bunks, grabbing their muskets, the half-dressed Federals rush into the night—ready for action. But the Southerners, slipping toward the powder magazine, apparently scouting to see if the old fort is garrisoned, vanish in the darkness, their footsteps resounding on the plank walk and then fade with the intruders into the hush of night. The smell of gunpowder is in the air. The shots are, without doubt, the first discharged in support of the Union; during the South's lightning maneuvers to grab Federal land and arms, the brief Barrancas encounter is the first successful resistance.

Now, heeding orders from Gen. Winfield Scott to protect government property, Slemmer spikes the Barrancas guns, and moves the powder and ammunition and his company of artillerists—reinforced by thirty ordinary seaman from the Navy Yard—across the bay to Fort Pickens on January 10.

The next day, Lt. Henry Erben of the store-ship *Supply* sacks Fort McRee on Foster's Bank (Perdido Key) and moves the powder to Pickens. Slemmer wants to destroy the Navy Yard magazine, but Armstrong declines, pleading lack of orders. For two days and nights in incessant rain, Slemmer's artillerists feverishly install the Pickens guns.

Two days later, 350 well-armed volunteers—five companies of Alabamians and one each from Pensacola and Santa Rosa County—march against the Navy Yard. Commodore Armstrong immediately surrenders. Quartermaster William Conway refuses to lower the United States flag during the surrender.

"I have served under that flag for forty years," Conway replies. "And I won't do it." Later, Conway wins a medal; Armstrong is court martialed.

But Pensacolian F. E. Renshaw, a Navy lieutenant, lowers the Stars and Stripes. On January 13 Colonel Chase's West Florida Army hoists its own American flag with one star; for Federals at Pickens it looks "like an old signal flag with a star put on it." It's symbolic of Florida's new emblem—thirteen stripes, alternate red and white, with a large white star in the center of a blue field.

Florida now holds the Gulf Coast's major naval prize, but with the Federals defending Fort Pickens the conquest is nullified—especially when Slemmer rejects three demands by Chase to surrender, and a quick assault is forestalled by the Pickens (or Buchanan) Truce. Florida Senator Stephen Russell Mallory joins with other Southerners, including Jefferson Davis and Judah P. Benjamin, in advising Governor Perry that possession of Pickens "is not worth one drop of blood to us . . . Bloodshed may be fatal to our cause."

Mallory, coming home after resigning his U.S.

Edward Aylesworth Perry, a brigadier general for the Confederacy, served as the governor of Florida from 1885-1889.
Pensacola Historical Society

Lt. Adam J. Slemmer, Federal defender of Fort Pickens.
T. T. Wentworth, Jr.

Senate seat, learns the U.S. steam sloop *Brooklyn* is transporting troops to Fort Pickens. Mallory wires President James Buchanan that no Florida militia attack would be made on the fort unless federal troops are landed. The president, unwilling to provoke military action in the South, still hoping for compromise with the secessionists, accepts Mallory's assurance and the *Brooklyn* remains off Pensacola harbor after its February 6 arrival. By February 19, with the *Sabine, St. Louis* and *Brooklyn* outside of the harbor and commanded by Captain Henry A. Adams, the troubled truce period becomes a slowing waiting game. Slemmer openly purchases food on the mainland and uses the Pensacola post office.

A month later, the Cotton States' delegates convene at Montgomery, form the Confederate States of America, drafting an interim constitution surprisingly a virtual duplicate of the one they had rejected, and choose Jefferson Davis provisional president. President Davis selects Mallory, whom he had known in the Senate, as Navy secretary. On March 11, 1861, a Davis friend from the Mexican War, Brig. Gen. Braxton Bragg, assumes command of Confederate troops in Mallory's truce-protected Pensacola, replacing Chase. For Charleston, Davis chooses P. G. T. Beauregard, the testy Louisiana Creole. Bragg and Beauregard commands are equal, for the only significant forts in the Confederacy still occupied by Federals were Pickens and Sumter, making either Pensacola or Charleston powder kegs for igniting war.

The Pickens truce, saving Buchanan from decision and cascading the problem into Lincoln's hands, gives the incoming president his first challenge of the impending crisis—and costs General Bragg an opportunity to clean out the nest of Federals preventing full mobilization of the major Confederate port.

For Lincoln, facing the decision to reinforce or abandon Fort Sumter, where Maj. Robert Anderson and his short-rationed garrison of eighty-five men held the world spotlight, the Fort Pickens crisis was seen as a tiny dot in the sea of secession. (But it was really a rattlesnake at the ankles of the president.)

The Confederate Congress, authorizing a provisional army of 10,500 officers and men, focuses on Pensacola and Charleston. The Confederate War Department says Bragg needs 5,000 men at Pensacola, where the North Carolinian is already constructing land batteries at Fort

Barrancas, Fort McRee, and the Navy Yard.

Bragg's 5,000 Florida, Alabama, Louisiana, and Mississippi soldiers drill and train in the sandy Warrington and Woolsey camps, decked in the bright attire of Southern Avengers, Alabama Invincibles, Orleans Cadets, Walton Guards, Crescent Rifles, Pensacola Guards and Rifle Rangers, and the Louisiana Chassuers.

Bragg's men pose for New Orleans photographer J. D. Edwards, New Hampshire-born, twenty-nine-year-old ambrotype portraitist, considered a pioneer cameraman of the Confederacy. In Pensacola, Edwards snaps some of the first military camp life images in the history of photography. He captures images of Cooper's Louisiana Zouave Battalion drilling on grounds of the Marine Barracks; the camp of the Orleans Cadets on Bayou Grande, just north of Warrington; the camps of the First Alabama and Ninth Mississippi regiments; the Spanish half-moon battery; sand batteries; and from atop the 165-foot lighthouse. His innovative work, preserved in Francis Trevelyan Miller's 1911 *Photographic History of the Civil War* and numerous books thereafter, provides a comprehensive panorama of the forts, guns, barracks, shipyards, and young men comprising Bragg's army.

English journalist William H. Russell of the *London Illustrated News* portrays Pensacola troops as long-bearded, wearing flannel shirts and slouched hats, "uniformless in all save brightly burnished arms and resolute purpose."

A New Orleans *Daily True Delta* correspondent, watching Federals swimming in the Santa Rosa Island surf, vents his Southern sympathy: "I saw the rogues polluting the waters of the island with their filthy carcasses. Where are the sharks—are they blocked out, too?"

Bragg, a dour martinet, astute drillmaster and disciplinarian, prepares for war. He's regular Army, a West Pointer, and a Mexican War hero, fabled for his successful command at Buena Vista ("A little more grape, Captain Bragg," Zachary Taylor had ordered at Buena Vista). He prohibits sale of alcoholic beverages, closes drinking saloons, whips his mostly civilian army into shape and builds mainland batteries, realizing Pickens cannot be taken without a regular siege. He displays a keen military mind and high moral character, yet his irascibility will later nullify his battlefield effectiveness. A baffling figure, Bragg antagonizes people repeatedly. In battle, especially at Chickamauga, he displays a bewildering personality; his victories are blunted by stubborn indecision and demoralizing incompetence. Yet, at Pensacola, Bragg's a hard-case disciplinarian, whipping a ragged mob of civilians into soldiers ready for their Shiloh baptism.

He takes advantage of the Pickens Truce to solidify defenses in anticipation of attacking Santa Rosa Island between April 12-15, 1861. Already President Davis, with little regard for the truce agreement, encourages Bragg to attack Pickens. But Bragg knows it will be a reckless assault, possibly an embarrassing failure.

During the early weeks of the truce, both sides strengthen defenses. With the warships *Sabine, St. Louis,* and *Brooklyn* outside the harbor, Pensacola is tense: Slemmer mounts guns on the Pickens ramparts, blocks casemate embrasures, and watches cautiously the Confederates strengthening Barrancas and McRee and building shore batteries.

Meanwhile, General Beauregard at Charleston warns the Federals that Fort Sumter would be stormed unless the post is peaceably surrendered.

Beauregard makes it clear Confederates would fire on Sumter if an attempt was made to provision and reinforce the Charleston bastion with troops and ammunition. The result would be civil war, of course.

But the Confederacy would bear the responsibility of firing the first shot. If Sumter yields to Confederate demands, then the Lincoln administration would be backing down; in effect, admitting inability to solve the crisis. Northern public opinion would not stand for that.

Then Lincoln moves—first he asserts federal authority by making a demonstration of strength at Fort Pickens. Pickens has not become the symbol of Sumter, due to its remote Gulf location from the Eastern states. But by making the Pensacola fort secure, he reasons the loss of Sumter can be charged to military necessity.

The North might accept that.

He orders two expeditions prepared—one for relief of Pickens, the other will stand by to reinforce and provision Sumter if circumstances warrant.

On March 12, Gen. Winfield Scott, commanding general of the U.S. Army, sends orders to Capt. Israel Vogdes at Fort Pickens to land his men and strengthen the island defenses. Vogdes asks Capt. Henry A. Adams, senior naval officer, for landing boats, but the captain refuses to believe the Pickens Truce has been terminated. He requests orders from Secretary of Navy Gideon

Commodore James Armstrong.
Mrs. Robert H. Weatherly photo

Stephen Russell Mallory.
Pensacola Historical Society

Welles. The delay sparks a near crisis; a Navy courier, Lt. John L. Worden, leaves Washington for Pensacola with secret orders.

On April 10, President Davis orders Beauregard to demand the surrender of Sumter; and as Major Anderson drafts his refusal, Lieutenant Worden, the Washington courier, arrives by train in Pensacola and obtains General Bragg's permission to go aboard the USS *Wyandotte* with orders of a "specific nature" on a "mission of mercy."

A storm delays Worden's oral communications of Welles' order directing the landing of Federal reinforcements until the next day, April 12—the date Beauregard's guns thunder over Fort Sumter at 4:30 in the morning.

Worden, shadowed by a Confederate officer, is arrested at Montgomery on his return train trip—the first prisoner of war. Later exchanged, Worden commands the U.S. ironclad *Monitor* in its Hampton Roads engagement with the CSS *Merrimack* or *Virginia*.

By midnight, a reinforcement detachment of five hundred soldiers, sailors and marines go ashore on Santa Rosa Island, completing Lincoln's Pickens-for-Sumter strategy.

Charleston guns rain hell over Fort Sumter; defeated and shaken Federals retreat to relief ships. Streets ring with wild shouts of joy as jubilant Southerners watch what the Confederate Secretary of State Robert Toombs of Georgia had warned would "inaugurate a civil war greater than any the world has yet known."

Pensacola's war moves to South Carolina. Despite desperate maneuvers, and a futile display of harbor fireworks, the Confederacy's flag is already descending at Pensacola.

The bombardment, momentarily expected, did not come for several months—and the nation's eyes are now on the western rivers and Tennessee and Virginia.

Bragg's troops lose the drydock when the tow line breaks and it floats into the hands of the Federals, who suspected it would be used as a floating battery against them. They burn it on September 2, 1861.

Federal raiders, one hundred sailors and marines commanded by Lt. John H. Russell, attacking on early morning darkness of September 13-14, burn the Confederate schooner *William P. Judah,* being outfitted as a privateer at the Navy Yard. Resisting valiantly, the Confederates are driven off by a boarding party in a fifteen-minute hand-to-hand combat producing the

war's first bloodshed in Florida—three federal marines killed, thirteen wounded; three defenders lose their lives.

As the Southerners watched the *Judah* sink off Fort Barrancas, they anxiously await Bragg's bombardment; but the Mexican War hero patiently continues consolidating his four-brigade command into two, led by Brig. Gen. Richard H. Anderson and Brig. Gen. Daniel Ruggles.

He then sends General Anderson on a Santa Rosa Island sortie, retaliating with a night landing with the aim of destroying Federal batteries that had been built outside Fort Pickens.

Anderson, commanding a thousand man expedition aboard Confederate steamers *Times* and *Neafie,* comes ashore four miles east of Fort Pickens at two o'clock in the morning and marches toward the fort in three columns, hoping to surprise the Federals. Plodding through sand, they burn the camp of Wilson's Zouaves (Sixth New York Volunteers) but are repulsed by regulars from the fort. Rushing to their landing boats, the Confederate night raiders return dejectedly to their camps on the mainland.

The Federal losses were 13 killed, 27 wounded, and 22 missing. Confederate casualties were 18 killed, 39 wounded, and 30 taken as prisoners.

Retaliating Federals begin a bombardment of Forts McRee and Barrancas on the mainland. Pickens guns and outlying batteries, assisted by cannon of the U.S. steamers *Niagara* and *Richmond* pepper the Confederate mainland batteries, silencing McRee before sunset on November 22. The guns continue the next day. In the afternoon, buildings in Warrington, near the Navy Yard, are in flames; the fires spread to the neighboring village of Woolsey. General Bragg, watching the smoke and cannon flame over the harbor, estimates the Federals fired five thousand times during the two-day bombardment, as compared with one thousand shots by his troops. Bragg ranks the heaviest bombardment in Florida history with the heaviest in the world, writing: "It was grand and sublime. The houses in Pensacola, ten miles off, trembled from the effect, and immense quantities of dead fish floated to the surface in the bay and lagoon, stunned by the concussion."

Another day of bombardment begins when a small vessel runs into the Navy Yard and draws Federal fire. Fort McRee explodes during the second exchange on January 1-2, 1862.

The Federals press for a combined operation to capture Pensacola, but lack naval forces; they unknowingly await the town's fate then being decided by events in Tennessee, where the South loses Forts Henry and Donelson and the long Blue line sweeps south on western rivers.

By January 1862, Bragg—promoted to major general and commanding western Florida and the entire state of Alabama—leads 18,214 men in the armies of Pensacola and Mobile. But Bragg—advocating a Napolenic strategy of rapid concentration and attack for the Confederacy—suggests abandoning Florida and Texas.

On February 8, 1862, Judah P. Benjamin, Confederate secretary of war, orders Bragg to rush all the troops he can spare to Tennessee, where Gen. Albert Sidney Johnston rallies a major army at Corinth, Mississippi, for what would be the Battle of Shiloh. On February 28, Bragg moves north from Mobile by the Mobile & Ohio Railroad, leading approximately ten thousand troops, described by an officer as "the finest and best disciplined body of troops the Confederacy ever had."

Remaining Confederates under Col. Samuel Jones carry out Bragg's orders to save the guns, torch the city, destroy all machinery, sawmills and lumber, and break up the railroad to the Junction, carrying the iron to a safe place. By May, the evacuation is complete; sheets of flame engulf Fort Barrancas, Fort McRee, and the marine hospital. Explosions shake the earth. North of the city raging fires, including a turpentine factory, cast an orange glow.

On the morning of May 10, 1862, Acting Mayor John Brosnaham surrenders Pensacola to U.S. Army Lt. Richard Jackson. Remnants of fleeing Confederate cavalry fire on the advanced guard as the thousand-man occupation force marches from Fort Barrancas, enters the city, and returns the Stars and Stripes to the Plaza Ferdinand flagstaff. The mayorship is offered to Phillip Caro, but he refuses; the Federals accept his recommendation, selecting Caro's son-in-law John Gormley mayor.

Federal Col. William (Billy) Wilson of the Sixth New York Infantry moves into the home of Stephen Mallory at 286 North Palafox Street, south of Gage Hill. And the Pensacolian, whose Pickens Truce had been a source of embarrassment, sets about building a Confederate Navy from Richmond while his wife, Angela Moreno Mallory's hometown becomes headquarters for the West Gulf Blockading Squadron.

The first District of Pensacola commander, Brig. Gen. Neal Dow, living in Colonel Chase's

The Confederate camp of the 9th Mississippi Regiment at Warrington Navy Yard was taken by the photographer of the Confederacy, J. D. Edwards in 1861.
Pensacola Historical Society

Burning the Pensacola Dry Dock off Fort Pickens on August 31, 1861. Harper's Weekly *print, October 12, 1861.*
T. T. Wentworth, Jr.

Sinking the Judah. Frank Leslie's Illustrated, *September 14, 1861.*
Pensacola Historical Society

home, quickly earns an infamous reputation for seizing furniture for private gain, especially pianos. Mary Caro Gormley writes in her diary that Dow "is not an honest man"—since eleven pianos and much furniture marked for shipment north is of dubious military importance. Union "Piano Raids" draw the wrath of New Orleans commander Benjamin Butler, who warns the plundered property belongs to the U.S. government.

Pensacolians, fleeing into Alabama, keep their municipal government alive by special Florida legislation that authorizes the Board of Aldermen to transact the city's business outside the corporate limits. Filo E. de la Rua, clerk of the circuit court, first moves city and county records and archives to Bluff Springs, thirty-five miles north along the Escambia River; then, with legislative approval, to Greenville, Alabama, where aldermen-in-exile, led by Mayor Francis B. Bobe, conduct public business and Pensacolians are allowed to buy and sell property in federally occupied Pensacola from mid-1862 until the surrender. At Greenville, alderman are Chairman George W. Hutton, Joseph Sierra, C. L. Le Baron, William H. Judah, James Knowles, Charles G. Barkley, and Benjamin Drake Wright.

The fleeing Rector of Christ Church, Dr. John Jackson Scott, who had served Bragg's army at Barrancas, establishes the Church of the Holy Comforter in Montgomery, providing spiritual comfort for Pensacolians-in-Alabama exile. And federal occupation troops quartered in Seville Square use his Pensacola church as barracks, hospital, and sometimes horse stable. Parish records of St. Johns Catholic Church of Warrington, moved to Pensacola during the bombardment, are also sent to Greenville.

Pensacola becomes a deserted city with weeds growing in the streets and in the ruins of burned brickyards, sawmills, and planing mills. On July 21, 1863, Dr. John Brosnham records only seventy-two whites and ten blacks in Pensacola, including Don Francisco Moreno, Spanish consul, staunch Confederate sympathizer and father-in-law of Stephen Mallory. Moreno, seventy, uses his flag of neutrality for protection of Southern marauders riding in and out of Pensacola frequently.

More than two thousand Pensacola refugees, destitute and homeless, fleeing raids by roving Confederate bands and counterattacks by Barrancas troops, crowd into "Shack Town" within picket lines of Fort Barrancas. The Federals feed the refugees and patrols sweep through the countryside for lumber, bricks, logs, windows, doors, and other building materials to erect the temporary sanctuary.

The *Pensacola Gazette,* dominant newspaper since 1824, passes from the scene by April 1861; but the *Tri-Weekly Observer,* published by M. F. Gonzalez, Frank Touart, and William H. Kirk, survives by pledging allegiance to the Union and earning the scorn of Pensacolians as a radical Republican sheet. Bragg has an *Observer* reporter "Nemo" arrested as Union spy.

By November 1863, ambitious Brig. Gen. Alexander Sandor Asboth, veteran of the 1848 Hungarian Revolution, is commander of the Pensacola district. He launches a series of raids, leading eleven hundred men north to Gonzalez, dislodging the Seventh Alabama Cavalry from Fort Hodgson and wounding thirty Confederates; and with a seven-hundred-man force—including black troops—sweeps across West Florida, engaging the two hundred men and boys of the "Cradle and Grave Militia Company" at the Battle of Marianna, September 26, 1864. Asboth, wounded in the face and arm at Marianna, returns to Barrancas with eighty-one prisoners, six hundred slaves, two hundred horses and mules, four hundred cattle, and seventeen wagons.

Outside the main theater of hostilities after the 1862 occupation, Pensacola's last contribution to the war is a 12,000-troop federal occupation army under Maj. Gen. Frederick Steele, marching from Fort Barrancas on March 20, 1865, for the land campaign against Mobile. Federals from Pensacola engage withering Confederate forces in the Battle of Spanish Fort on the heights overlooking the Alabama port city. But, much like Pensacola's earlier role, the massive encounter is overshadowed by events elsewhere, specifically the April 9, 1865 surrender of Robert E. Lee and the Army of Northern Virginia at Appomattox.

By April 20, Federal forces enter Greenville, Alabama—the day Greenville's Pensacolians end their exiled government and look south to home and rebuilding. On May 20, federal troops enter Tallahassee, ending the Confederacy in Florida.

Among Pensacola's war heroes, Edward A. Perry converts the Pensacola Rifle Rangers into Company A, Second Florida Infantry and earns his brigadier stars fighting at Yorktown, Williamsburg, Richmond, Sharpsburg, Fredericksburg, Chancellorsville, and the Wilderness, where he was severely wounded and disabled. He serves with reserve forces in Alabama until the surrender.

Returning to Pensacola, Brig. Gen. Perry launches a successful law practice and political career. In 1885 he becomes the first Pensacolian elected Florida governor, the fourteenth, serving until 1889. His home at Wright and Palafox streets—today the Scottish Rite Temple—is the scene for Governor Perry's grand parties during an administration that leads Florida to adopt a new Constitution and establish a State Board of Education.

General Perry's dream—a Confederate Monument for Florida, with the people of Florida contributing funds for the memorial—becomes a Pensacola reality in 1891, two years after his death. Led by Mrs. Edward A. Perry and Mrs. William Dudley Chipley, the campaign attracts most of the funds from Escambia County. Perry's friend and political ally, former Confederate Lieutenant Colonel W. D. Chipley, encourages the placement of the granite monument on Palafox (Gage) Hill as centerpiece for Florida Square, renamed Lee Square in honor of the commander of the Army of Northern Virginia. The stone soldier atop the columnar monument is an adaption of Eagen's painting, *After Appomattox,* hanging in the Virginia capitol in Richmond; his pedestal honors the uncrowned heroes of the Southern Confederacy, CSA president Jefferson Davis and two Pensacolians—General Perry, commander of the Florida Brigade under General Lee, and Confederate Secretary of the Navy Stephen Mallory. Perry is buried in St. Johns Cemetery, along with Confederate Generals William Miller and Samuel Gibbs French.

Revered by Pensacolians as the husband of Angela Sylvania Moreno, and criticized for Southern seaport losses, Stephen Mallory proves an innovative Confederate Navy secretary who encourages the new naval technology—ironclad vessels, submarines, and torpedoes—during the four years of the Confederacy. As a Pensacola lawyer and pre-war U.S. Senator, Mallory had married Angela, eldest of twenty-seven children sired by one of Pensacola's patriarchs, Francisco Moreno. She is six years old when the Floridas become American, speaking only Spanish until entering boarding school. As a Confederate cabinet officer's wife, the socially-minded, strong-willed Angela Mallory is a popular Richmond hostess, entertaining President Davis and Confederate officials, including Mobile's Adm.

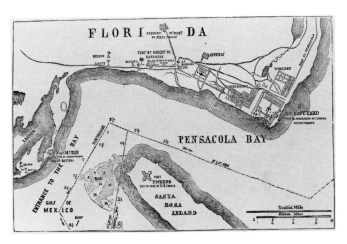

This map shows the harbor of Pensacola and the location of military installations. Harper's Weekly *print, February 9, 1861.*
Pensacola Historical Society

Col. William (Billy) Wilson, commander of the U.S. Fifth New York on Santa Rosa Island.
T. T. Wentworth, Jr.

Raphael Semmes.

Arrested in May 1865 during Davis' flight from Richmond after Appomattox, Stephen Mallory is imprisoned in Fortress Monroe eleven months until President Andrew Johnson signs his parole in 1866. He and Angela return to Pensacola, where he resumes the practice of law. Well-respected, Mallory urges full allegiance to the national government, and feels strongly blacks should enjoy equality under the law. He dies on November 9, 1873, and is buried in St. Michael's Cemetery. His son, Stephen R. Mallory II, emerges as a Pensacola journalist and politician, following his father to the U.S. Senate in 1897.

Historians argue the Sumter-for-Pickens theory, acknowledging that it could have been Pensacola and not Charleston. They contend President Davis hoped to do at Pickens what Lincoln has been accused of doing at Sumter—maneuvering the other side to fire the first shot.

Regardless, the war came at Charleston; yet it could have been ignited by events in Pensacola—*and may have been;* Slemmer's bold action helped the Federals keep the Stars and Stripes over Pickens throughout the war.

The war came through the first overt Confederate act at Charleston because Montgomery's war department was neither subtle enough nor strong enough to focus sufficient firepower on the tiny island command at Pensacola.

Nonetheless, the *first shots* at Fort Barrancas, the events-shaping Pickens Truce, and the Sumter-for-Pickens political decision in Washington assure Pensacola of its vital first-act role in the nation's most profound national experience.

Under military rule until 1868, when Congress accepts Florida's new Constitution and Third Military District Commander George Meade withdraws Federal troops, Pensacola's bitter war wounds are deep; houses, businesses, and Navy Yard in shambles, slavery investments depleted, moderate Republicans dominating politics despite the aggressiveness of *Observer* Editor William J. Kirk. Twice Kirk challenges former Confederate Navy Secretary Stephen Mallory to a duel, the second accepted by the well-respected lawyer but averted when both men are arrested.

Newly freed blacks, seeking help from the Freedman's Bureau, stir fear; fights are frequent—but former slaves in Pensacola fare better than most tortured Reconstruction regions of the South. Union supporter Alexander C. Blount records blacks and whites are treated equally in county courts.

Only a few military personnel remain at harbor installations; yet by the end of the decade several hundred freedman work at the Navy Yard. And Pensacolians are rebuilding, finding new economic life in lumber and trade. By early 1866, shipments of yellow pine go to England and Europe. In 1867 the first post-war American ship transports lumber to Boston. Once again Pensacolians turn to the bay, and the emerging sawmill industry in the West Florida woods, hoping port shippers and the newly organized workingman's association of stevedores will bring a forest of sailing ships into Pensacola harbor.

Scene of Spanish failure and victory, French ambitions, British neglect, and now shattered Southern dreams, Pensacola in the 1870s and 1880s turns to city building, marine commerce, and railroad building—guided by the abundance of yellow pine standing verdant across the untapped West Florida wilderness.

Battle of Santa Rosa Island. Harper's
Weekly, December 7, 1861.
Pensacola Historical Society

Brig. Gen. Neal Dow of piano raid
fame. General Dow, while in command at Pensacola, developed a great
fondness for pianos and
articles of furniture. "Piano raids" to
nearby areas just about left Western
Florida devoid of fine furniture. It
was reported that the rebels offered
to exchange him for six pianos, but
he was later exchanged in the regular
manner.
Pensacola Historical Society

Gen. Braxton Bragg, Confederate
commander at Pensacola.
Pensacola Historical Society

Angela Moreno, daughter of Don
Francisco Moreno, married Stephen
Russell Mallory, Secretary of the Con-
federate Navy. They lived in Key
West during the early years of their
marriage.
Pensacola Historical Society

This photograph from atop Fort Barrancas was taken by J. D. Edwards in 1861.
Pensacola Historical Society

Major General Samuel Gibbs French is one of four Confederate leaders buried in Pensacola. The others are Generals William Miller and Edward A. Perry, and Navy Secretary Stephen R. Mallory.
Pensacola Historical Society

William Miller, a Pensacola Confederate general, is seen here in his later years.
Pensacola Historical Society

Marine Terminus Railroad, circa 1877.
Pensacola Historical Society

P A R T

8

Bonanza on the Bay

After Appomattox and miseries of the Reconstructed South, drumbeats of sectional conflict subside; near the bayfront, Pensacolians hear the machinery of promised prosperity as railroads bring yellow pine from the West Florida and South Alabama interior:

From the sawmill-deck, constant assaults of escaping stream push the carriage; the rumble and roar of unseen forces crash through the massive framework. Vibrating, the steam-nigger turns a heavy yellow pine log and snugs it back against the headblocks. Then a steady chop-chop of metal saws converts a four-inch flitch into ten or a dozen boards. Now yelping butting-saws and trimmers, animated by pulleys, gears, live-rolls and idlers, bring sweet sounds of Pensacola's timber industry during the last quarter of the nineteenth century.

The sound of crosscut saws felling pine heightens the economic drama of the West Florida pineywoods—accelerated by millmen from Michigan and other lumbering states seeking profit from an untapped wilderness during Pensacola's boom years of the 1870s and 1880s. They turn Pensacola's post-war economic lifeblood into a world wide business.

Europeans, experiencing an industrial revolution feeding a housing boom, create a hungry market perfectly timed for West Florida with the world's great stands of yellow pine ripe for cutting.

Pensacola, virtually a ghost town during the war years, beckons; population doubles to eight thousand—half the influx black—five years after Appomattox. Pensacola Telegraph Company lines, complete in 1866, link the city with the interior; pineywoods sawmills spring up in surrounding woodlands. The Hyer family, which had acquired a pre-Civil War lumber fortune in the West Florida woods, opens a timber and ship brokerage and soon are servicing shippers' banking and financial transactions. Businessmen organize the Pensacola City Company to feed a budding real estate market. They herald "opportunities for young men of energy and intellect to build up a splendid future are unsurpassed by those of any place in America and rivaled by those of any port on the Southern coast."

Despite yellow fever epidemics, the nationwide Panic of 1873 that closed mills and businesses, and unrest caused by American laborers and Canadian migrants competing for work at port wharves and lumber mills, the city economy reawakens by mid-decade. The sleepy, war-wracked backwoods town envisions boom years after the railroad to Montgomery is rebuilt by 1870.

77

Again, desire for annexation surfaces in Alabama and in West Florida. Colonel A. C. Blount and Republican leader George E. Wentworth lead the movement heavily favored in Pensacola because of the potential of connecting the port with Alabama's coal fields, iron mines, cotton land, and city markets. But other Floridians oppose the scheme, eventually killing the proposal.

With the beginning of the logging railroad era, and the emergence of a former Confederate colonel from Columbus, Georgia, in the 1880s, Pensacolians find confidence for the post-Civil War claim their harbor city will become the "Future Commercial Emporium of the Southern states."

Lumber. Railroads.

Once isolated, now with track north and east linking centers of commerce, Pensacola finds its post-Reconstruction destiny as deep-water port anointed the Yellow Pine Capital of the World during the bonanza of the last quarter of the nineteenth century.

William Henry Chase's railroad dream becomes reality the year of his death—1870. The newly chartered Pensacola & Louisville Railroad Company gains control of the old Alabama & Florida Company property and rebuilds the track, linking with the Mobile & Montgomery Railroad at Pensacola Junction (Flomaton), six miles south of war-ravaged Pollard. Pensacolians named Chase Street for the New Englander who had worked for timber rail lines now emerging. The six-mile Pensacola & Perdido is hauling tonnage from the Muscogee and Millview lumber operations to port wharves in 1873; and a spur line connects the Navy Yard.

Yet the fort builder, Southern militia commander, and Pensacola visionary lives to see newer generations give Pensacola a permanent interstate connection with rails now crisscrossing the Reconstruction South.

But it is former Confederate Lt. Col. William Dudley Chipley, at age thirty-six scarred by war and tormented by Georgia Reconstruction, who casts a long shadow on Pensacola after his arrival in December 1876 as manager of the Pensacola & Louisville Railroad. Beset by faltering management, the P & L looks to Chipley to strengthen the war-shattered, bankrupt-crippled and now reconditioned railroad. He delivers the road to Louisville & Nashville stockholders.

Skillful manager, astute politician, and tireless promoter of Pensacola, Chipley brings Pensacola a new spirit and vision: he reasons railroad ex-

pansion would negate the annexation argument. In September 1877, Chipley writes an illustrated booklet on Pensacola and West Florida surroundings, naming his adopted city "The Naples of America" and extolling the natural beauty, history, agricultural and timber resources, and the geography of West Florida and its nearness to Mobile, New Orleans, and the "resorts of the Gulf Coast." In the mid-1880s his *Facts About Florida* heralds Pensacola's and West Florida's potential for tourism, new residents, and business investors. During the next twenty-one years—until his death in 1897—the leadership of the man revered as "Mr. Railroad of West Florida" significantly alters the economic course of the seaport and opens West Florida for new milltowns and harvest of yellow pine and naval stores.

After 1883, when rails were joined at River Junction on the Apalachicola River, the Pensacola & Atlantic ties the Panhandle with Peninsula Florida. Between Milton, east of Escambia Bay, and Marianna, the cotton center for fertile Jackson County, new towns—Crestview, DeFuniak Springs, Caryville, Bonifay, Chipley—rise along the rails threading 161 miles through virgin long-leaf pine forests.

First reorganizing the road into the Pensacola Railroad Company, Chipley shares with L & N officials the vision of bridging the West Florida pinelands, tapping the lucrative interior, and linking with rails to the Atlantic Ocean.

But Chipley brings more to Pensacola than railroads. Born in Columbus, Georgia, in 1840, he grew up in Lexington, Kentucky, as the son of a Baptist minister. Schooled at Kentucky Military Institute and Transylvania University, Chipley commands Kentucky troops. Wounded at Shiloh, Chickamauga, and Atlanta, Chipley is captured by Gen. William T. Sherman's Union forces and imprisoned at Johnson's Island until Appomattox.

Returning to Columbus, where he marries a Georgia planter's daughter, Ann Elizabeth Billips, Chipley emerges as a Georgia Democratic party leader. Chipley attains national attention when arrested as one of twelve suspects in the murder of Georgia scalawag George W. Ashburn, who is slain by masked men, presumably Ku Kluxers, in a black Columbus brothel in 1868. Chipley is imprisoned at Fort Pulaski, triggering Georgia howls of miscarriage of justice; he endures a conspiracy trial with former Confederate Vice President Alexander (Little Aleck) Stephens defending him against prosecutor

Joseph E. Brown, rabid States Righter and Civil War governor of Georgia. The infamous Ashburn Affair trial ends abruptly without resolution when Georgia ratifies the Fourteenth Amendment.

His investments depleted, Chipley becomes a general agent for the Baltimore & Ohio Railroad—experience he brings to Pensacola two years later as general manager of the struggling Pensacola-to-Montgomery road.

Although Pensacola shippers and sawmills produce logs and lumber from river-rafted timbers to vessels in port, the undeveloped frontier leads Chipley and other Escambians to believe the harbor will become the main Gulf port for Alabamians as well as West Florida. Chipley has a bigger vision; West Florida will develop as a major part of the state if the woodlands are bridged by rails from Pensacola to Jacksonville, with the Tallahassee connection then being completed from Quincy to the eastern bank of the Apalachicola River at Chattahoochee.

Chipley begins a race with East Florida railroad barons Henry Flagler and Henry Plant to acquire millions of acres of state and federal land grants available to entrepreneurs rebuilding and expanding the state's railway system. He claims the P & A share—3,888,600 acres, with 1,700,000 east of the Apalachicola, extending from the river to the Atlantic Ocean. Chipley sees the vast acreage for West Florida development, harvesting pine, and turpentine when the L & N gains control of the P & A on May 1881; he controls the railroad expansion as vice president and general superintendent.

The P & A builds the steepled, Victorian-styled Union Depot at the Y-junction of L & N and P & A trackage on the northeast corner of Tarragona and Wright streets. Crews lay track eastward out of the city and across the marshy mouth of Bayou Texar and along the curving shore of the red-clay bluffs to stations Bohemia and Bellevue and the Escambia Bay bridge (Yneistra).

The freight depot rises three blocks south of Union Depot on Garden Street with spur tracks southeast to the corner of Garden and Alcaniz streets. East of Union Depot, on the main line, the P & A builds engine and freight-car sheds, turn table, and other facilities connecting with spur lines veering southeast to Muscogee Wharf.

From 1881 to 1883 more than twenty-two

hundred men hack through forest and swamp, bridging Escambia Bay and the West Florida rivers and streams, spiking three-thousand cross ties to the mile to connect 161 miles of track from Pensacola eastward to the Apalahicola River. On August 15, 1882, the first passenger train passes over the Escambia Bay bridge on a maiden excursion for Pensacola dignitaries to Milton and the Yellow River pine-forest country. Leaving the Union Depot, passengers stop at Magnolia Bluff, the new P & A resort and pavilion built on the red cliffs of what will become East Pensacola Heights. When excursionists reach Garcon peninsula in Santa Rosa County, former Confederate Brig. Gen. Edward A. Perry leads "three cheers and a tiger" for Chipley. On the return trip to Pensacola, the train is halted in the middle of the wooden bridge, and passengers hoist champagne glasses, toasting what Circuit Court Judge Augustus E. Maxwell heralds as the "greatest event in the history of Pensacola."

In April 1883, beginning with Engineer Peter (Pete) W. Kelly making the first "Blue Ribbon Run" passenger run from Pensacola to Jacksonville, Chipley's railroad was opening the woodlands for timbering and the Pensacola port for business at the L & N wharves.

The Louisville & Nashville absorbs the independent Pensacola & Atlantic in 1885, elevating E. O. Saltmarsh to Pensacola superintendent and designating Chipley land commissioner. The Georgian devotes his energies to city building, acquiring railroad grants and selling acreage to sawmill and turpentine investors, and promoting the city and its commerce as president of the Pensacola Board of Trade and the first president of the Pensacola Chamber of Commerce in 1889. Chipley acquires one-fifteenth of the entire state—2,830,619 acres—for the L & N financiers. Even though he yields to the Florida Railroad Company of former U.S. Senate David Yulee for lands east of the Apalachicola, Chipley proves successful in his race with Flagler and Plant.

Chipley lobbies for reopening the Navy Yard and deepening the port with hopes of home-porting portions of the Atlantic fleet in Pensacola harbor. He urges construction of public buildings and works for free postal service. As railroader and tourism promoter, Chipley helps organize the annual Florida Chautauqua at Lake DeFuniak, named for Col. Fred de Funiak, L & N general manager and first president of the P & A railroad.

With manufactured goods, fertilizer, coal, cotton, and agricultural products flowing with timber from the rails to the L & N port wharves, Chipley leads efforts to increase the coal-car fleet, dredge Pensacola harbor, and improve Muscogee Wharf for coal and fertilizer handling. L & N helps form the Export Coal Company which becomes the Gulf Transit Company in 1895. Tarragona Wharf is reconditioned and enlarged and the one-hundred-acre switching and marshaling yard at Goulding is built in 1896 in anticipation of a major Navy fleet stationed in Pensacola harbor. L & N's thriving port commerce at its Commendencia, Tarragona, and Muscogee wharves coincides with Colonel Chipley's rise as a political powerbroker, mayor, and state senator; and by the 1890s, he is ambitious for the Washington seat held by U.S. Senator Wilkinson Call, nephew of Territorial Governor Richard Keith Call.

On sandy Pensacola streets, during the Chipley years leading to a new century, a new commercial city arises with a building boom animated by bankers, financial houses, Florida's first savings and loan association, streetcar lines, electricity for illumination, a sewage system, telephones, new neighborhoods, a new city government, and the city's first permanent daily newspapers, the Chipley-inspired *Daily News* in 1889, and Frank L. Mayes' progressive competitor, *The Pensacola Journal* in 1898.

In the 1880s, more sailing masts fill the bay. And with the vessels come Europeans—many remaining to enrich the ethnic flavor of the working man's economy enlivening the waterfront. From the blue water of the bay north and east, Pensacola runs from the canvas of sailing ships to the woodsmoke of railroad engines. All roads—those sand-rutted with wagon wheels; those spiked with iron rails for the steam monsters snorting power in the West Florida woods—lead to the waterfront.

Lumber from bayfront docks go into black, capricious holds of full-rigged sailing ships, barks, brigantines, and schooners for a steady river of yellow pine flowing across oceans to England, Europe, South Africa, and Central and South America.

Stevedores load timber from rebuilt port wharves; beyond, in the bay, a forest of sailing canvas rides the tides. A fleet of steam tugs maneuver hundreds of schooners, brigs, barks—vessels from Russia, Denmark, Germany, England, France, Spain, Norway, Italy, and Austra-

lia. Crews fill the ships' bellies with lumber by cutting *trap doors* in the bow just above the water's edge, sealing them and cutting others upward until the cargo is completed.

Waters beyond the bay offers another harvest. In the late 1860s, Yankee fishermen work the Gulf for red snapper, including New Englander Sewell C. Cobb, who forecasts the future by organizing the Pensacola Fish Company in 1869. Two years later another New Englander, Andrew Fuller Warren, joins Cobb's firm; so does fisherman Thomas E. Welles. They rely on New England captains for fishing vessels until 1879, when the company develops its own fleet of schooners. Men of the sea, harvesting the fertile waters within fifteen miles of Pensacola, call their sailing vessels *smacks* for the smacking sound of salt water filling the open wells to preserve fresh catches.

In 1880 Warren forms the rival Warren and Company; two years later Welles and Eugene Edwin Saunders feed the growing market with the third fishing business partnership, E. E. Saunders Company. With rail connections north, the fishing companies along the waterfront supply cities across the United States. In the mid-1890s, the Pensacola-owned fishing companies employ almost five hundred men, harvesting almost 100 percent of the commercial supply. During winter months, Warren and Sanders crews fill their vessels on the snapper-rich Campeche Banks off Mexico four hundred miles southeast of Pensacola. Tons of snapper, grouper, scamp, red fish, pompano, trout, Spanish mackerel, and mullet pour into bellies of Pensacola-owned fishing vessels for fish-processing houses along the bayfront. Thirty years after Appomattox, Pensacola is known as the Snapper Capital of the World. Manufactured ice in the late 1880s substantially reduces costs and expands markets. In 1885 more than three million tons of fish leave Pensacola wharves.

Fishing captains often hire crew "volunteers" after long nights in waterfront saloons by supplying beer and whiskey to prevent hangover horrors at sea.

Warren and Saunders companies ship $600,000 worth of red snapper across the nation in 1904 in refrigerated railroad cars. In 1916 there are thirty-five Greek fishing vessels in Pensacola. The Warren and Saunders companies control snapper harvests into the twentieth century until overfishing, depletion of the Campeche harvest, and the fleet-and dock-damaging 1906 and 1916

An 1874 woodcut view of the port from South Palafox shows the many sailing ships arriving to export the hewn timbers harvested from the nearby forests.
Pensacola Historical Society

This later view of Palafox, circa 1894, is looking north from Government Street at Plaza Ferdinand. There has been much speculation concerning the use of the platform seen in the northwest corner of the Plaza.
Pensacola Historical Society

Col. William Dudley Chipley.
Pensacola Historical Society

Pensacola & Perdido Railroad Wharf in the 1870s.
Florida State Archives

hurricanes sharply diminish the industry before World War I.

But E. E. Saunders is more than a fishing company tycoon; he develops a lucrative market for roadbuilders as contractor for millions of tons of ballast—rock, tile, sand, gavel—used to stabilize empty sailing ships during long Atlantic voyages. Ships entering Pensacola harbor dump the ballast in cribs at the Deer Point Quarantine Station and along the bay shoreline. But since vessel owners must pay for off-loading ballast, frequent illegal shoreline dumpings eventually create almost sixty acres of "Made Land." Five million tons of ballast for ships from across the world expand the shoreline south of present-day Main Street.

Merchants and lumber barons push the city north beyond the Old Spanish neighborhood near the bay. They move up *the Hill,* converting yellow pine and cypress into elegantly fili-greed Queen Anne style houses with broad verandas, shady balconies, and ornate turrets in the city's first neighborhoods of affluence—later christened North Hill. Centered around the homes of Henry Baars and W. D. Chipley, the Hill becomes the favored place for ship brokers, lumber merchants, and professional men. Looking down Palafox Street, middle-class inhabitants are near their businesses yet remote from the noise, crowds, and roistering behavior in saloons and brothels of the working man's waterfront. As expected, it becomes "Snob Hill"; the other Pensacolians are convinced Hill inhabitants "look down" on the rest of the city.

In 1885, Dr. James S. Herron—medical pioneer sharing Pensacola's early hospital development and battles with yellow fever with Navy surgeon Isaac Hulse and Dr. Robert B. S. Hargis—builds the most visible North Hill home—a two and one-half story, fifteen-room Queen Anne style house—atop ancient ruins of British-built Fort George. Gage Hill is still pocked with gun emplacements from the Civil War period. The legendary Herron house mirrors attitudes of North Hill business leaders: large, comfortable, yet not overly ostentatious. It stands until 1963, serving as the headquarters for the Pensacola Council of Knights of Columbus, which replaced the landmark with a new council hall.

Spreading north, around Gage Hill, the elite neighborhood obscures the torn ground, redoubts, and entrenchments of the 1781 Span-

ish-British battlefield. Other middle-class residents move toward Bayou Texar, giving shape to the East Hill neighborhood north of the Pensacola & Atlantic railroad tracks; others settle across Texar in what will become East Pensacola Heights.

Near the waterfront, Europeans group in ethnic neighborhoods: "Little Italy" between Barcelonia and Coyle streets from Garden to Main; "Little Norway" from A and G streets south to Main Street. The Scandinavian Missionary Society of Norway erects the Norwegian Seaman's church at Palafox and Pine streets, probably the first in the United States for Scandinavian seamen. Its cross-laden spire rises above the bustling waterfront of wooden piers, fish houses, ship stores, saloons, sawmills, and grocery stores along wagon-rutted streets leading to wooden wharves.

The Irish settle in Woolsey and Warrington, working at the Navy Yard, on the docks and in lumber mills; German and Austrian Jews enter retail and wholesale business, and the Reformed Jews organize the Beth-el Congregation—Florida's first—in 1876 and erect the state's first Jewish temple on East Chase Street in 1895.

The Jews organize their own social organization, the Progress Club, first located above the Opera House, then established on West Chase Street between Baylen and Palafox in 1909. The city's prosperous businessmen socialize, dine, and discuss business and politics at the Osceola Club, founded in 1872 by the LeBaron and Gonzalez families. In 1883, the social and reading club develops large and lavish quarters in the Brent Building on Palafox Street. Businessmen and political leaders relax in the lavish atmosphere of art-lined walls, Italian marble tables, and silk-upholstered furniture. At the Bayshore, west of Pensacola, the Country Club provides exclusive recreation for members in the 1880s.

The bustling export business spawns businesses near the bayfront—barrel makers, sail makers, ship chandlers, bankers, mercantile operators, and grocers such as Bavarian-born Alabamian Lewis Bear, Confederate Army veteran who moves from Greenville in 1876 to open a retail grocery on Intendencia and Barcelonia streets. The Lewis Bear emporium, later fronting Plaza Ferdinand, expands into a regional wholesale-distributing company with downtown warehouses near the bayfront. A century later the Lewis Bear Company is one of Florida's largest operations carrying the legacy as Pensacola's oldest

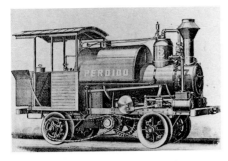

The Perdido "Pole Road" Engine was developed for use on rails made of tree trunks laid out in the remote harvesting areas.
Pensacola Historical Society

Pensacola, Mobile & New Orleans Railroad engine.
Pensacola Historical Society

Mrs. W. D. Chipley (Elizabeth Billups, known as Bettie to her friends) encouraged her husband to contribute to the city's improvement. Bettie was an active member and fundraiser for the First Baptist Church.
Photo courtesy of First Baptist Church

Union Depot of the Louisville & Nashville Railroad, circa 1900.
Pensacola Historical Society

continuing business operation with a multi-state mercantiling operation.

Black craftsmen—carpenters, blacksmiths, plasterers and bricklayers, tinners, cigar makers, shoemakers, cabinet makers—feed the economy along with unskilled laborers. Black residences and churches spring up across the city, with concentrations along the railroad tracks, near the business district and in the Belmont-Devilliers neighborhood southwest of North Hill. Successful blacks emerge with their special identity—John Sunday serves in the Florida legislature in 1874 and as a city alderman from 1878 to 1881; D. J. Cunningham operates the Excelsior Grocery in 1895; and attorney Thomas DeSalle Tucker and entrepreneur Alexander Plummer invest in black-owned businesses.

Pensacola's Creoles, whose ancestry is a blend of Spanish, French, Canary Islanders, free persons of color, and former slaves, retain their identity apart from the black population. Many are professionals, artisans, craftsmen, and barbers listed in the city directory as "white" or "Creole" before "Jim Crow" laws force the Creoles to choose between calling themselves white or black. Regarding themselves as a distinct cultural entity—tracing their ancestry in the city more than one hundred years—the Creoles form a closely-knit society. They live near their church, St. Joseph's Catholic Church on Government Street, and socialize in the St. Michael's Benevolent Social Club, Creole Mutual Aid and Benevolent Association, and the Creole Catholic Benevolent Association, established between 1878 and 1901. Their heritage is symbolized by preservation of the Creole Benevolent Society meeting house on East Government Street near Seville Square.

Constantine Apostolou Panagiotou sails from the island of Skopelos in 1865 to become Pensacola's first permanent Greek resident. And soon others, led by Constantine's brother Nicholas and nephew Paul Liollio, begin the Skopelos migration for Pensacola's small residential enclave. Greeks work as red snapper fishermen and carpenters; operate grocery stores and fruitstands, and begin Pensacola's Greek restaurant tradition. Constantine and Nicholas Americanize their name to Apostle; in 1887-1888 Constantine Apostle becomes the first person of Greek ancestry to be elected public official in the United States, serving one term as Pensacola mayor. Nicholas and Paul Liollio lead the Greek restaurant tradition with their successful Nick's Restaurant and Saloon at 211 South Palafox Street. The growing Greek community keeps its national and cultural heritage alive with the goal of a place of worship, a reality on Garden Street in 1910 with the opening of the Annunciation Greek Orthodox Church. In 1903, Greeks own twenty of the thirty retail fruit stores in Pensacola.

Constantine and Nicholas Apostle's descendants continue Pensacola's Greek restaurant tradition in the twentieth century, symbolized by John A. Liollio's Garden Street restaurant and another named for their native land, Skopelos Restaurant.

The Pensacola Gas Company lights the city streets, and promotes the Welsbach Lamp for homes, but new illumination is in the future when the first electric light glows in Pensacola at 7:00 p.m. on December 10, 1888. Soon the Pensacola Electric Light and Power Company—founded in 1887, five years after Thomas Edison turned on the first light for public use—is firing coal-burning boilers for steam at the city's first power plant near Baylen and Cedar streets. Electricity is primarily for businesses—hotels, ice manufacturing—with excess sold to nearby customers. Power is available generally during early evening hours before the more modern electric plant is built at Barracks and Main Street. Electricity soon transforms the horse and mule-drawn vehicles of the Pensacola Street Car Company, started in July 1884 by Conrad Kupfrian, Henry Pfeiffer and John Cosgrove. Beginning at Palafox Street Wharf, trolley tracks run north to Wright Street and the Union Depot, west to Moreno Street and Kupfrian's Park, a popular picnic and fairgrounds near present-day Baptist Hospital.

Pensacola's early development of an electrical system is linked with expansion of the street railway business. In 1892, the expanded trolley line runs track for the steam-power streetcar "Dummy Line" along the Bayshore and across Bayou Chico and Bayou Grande to Woolsey and Warrington. In the 1890s, electricity and compressed air replace horse power, and the expanded street railway system in the new century causes Pensacolians to spread out into East Pensacola Heights, Lakeview subdivision in East Hill, and West Pensacola (Brownsville).

Several power company mergers mark Pensacola's experimental era of electrical power when small facilities generate power for ice-making, sawmills, and transit systems. The Pensacola Electric Company, organized in 1906, acquires

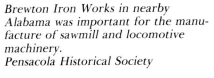

Brewton Iron Works in nearby Alabama was important for the manufacture of sawmill and locomotive machinery.
Pensacola Historical Society

Two men handle a cross-cut saw in the harvesting of the pines near Pensacola.
Pensacola Historical Society

Many logs were loaded on railroad cars to be taken to the mills for processing.
Pensacola Historical Society and T. T. Wentworth, Jr.

Special logging trains were used to transport the logs from the West Florida and Alabama camps to the mills.
Pensacola Historical Society

the railway company—the first to operate the trolley system and generate power. Transferred to Southeastern Power and Light Company in 1925, the Pensacola Electric Company is a direct ancestor of Gulf Power Company, which serves more than 245,000 customers in ten West Florida counties as a subsidiary of the multi-state Southern Company a century later.

Organized on November 22, 1925, Gulf Power Company absorbs the Pensacola Electric Company in 1926, and inherits the public transit system with thirty cars annually transporting more than a million passengers. In 1931, the automobile makes the electric trolley obsolete; Gulf Power turns to expanding power lines across Escambia County and West Florida.

In the last quarter of the twentieth century Gulf Power emerges as a major West Florida industry, promoter of Pensacola and regional economic development and active corporate citizen. In the 1980s the company builds its $25 million Hawkshaw corporate headquarters building on a thirteen-acre historical site overlooking Bayfront Parkway and Pensacola Bay. The five-story, L-shaped building, nestled with the natural contour of the old Hawkshaw community, preserves the archaeological and historical legacies of aboriginal life and early Colonial Pensacola. A neighborhood in the nineteenth and early twentieth centuries, the Hawkshaw historical site represents the British period as the site of the villa or summer residence of Royal Governor Peter Chester in the 1770s.

The steady crack of carpenter's hammers in 1881 inspires Scotsman Thomas C. Watson to organize the Pensacola Building and Loan Association—Florida's first—and the Workingman's Building and Savings Association two years later. Watson's theory was collecting in comparatively small sums weekly or monthly from a large number of people and loan to others with approved security either to build homes, enter business or other purposes.

The Pensacola builder and developer envisions regular, systematic, and compulsory savings, joining S. S. Harvey, Henry Horsler, L. P. Knowles, J. S. Leonard, John Cosgrove, B. R. Pitt, and James M. Hilliard to give birth to the building association idea.

In 1889, merger of the two associations provide the foundation for Mutual Loan and Savings Association, spawning West Florida's largest savings institution in the twentieth century. Known as Mutual Building and Savings Associa-

tion in 1922, it's federally chartered as Mutual Federal Savings and Loan Association in 1952, and becomes the state-chartered First Mutual Savings Association in 1981. Generations of the Watson and Blount families pioneer the association, including Capt. James C. Watson, grandson of founder Thomas C. Watson, and A. C. (Clement) Blount, grandson of Judge A. C. Blount.

In 1960, with Clement Blount chairman of the board, Mutual Federal relocates in a new North Baylen Street building and expands branch offices in four West Florida counties. A. C. Blount, Thomas C. Watson, E. W. Hopkins, W. G. Champlin, and former Mayor Barney Burks, Jr., serve as presidents during the growth years leading to new ownership by AmSouth Bancorporation of Birmingham. On November 1, 1987, First Mutual becomes AmSouth Bank of Florida, continuing the legacy of Mutual's 1960s-1980s slogan, "Building Pensacola."

Confederate veteran Francis Celestino Brent joins with Louis and William Knowles in 1876 to establish the Knowles and Brent Bank, leading the race of lumbermen and entrepreneurs to form local banking institutions to meet demands of increasing commerce. But the partnership dissolves in 1880, and the Knowles brothers unite with Daniel F. Sullivan to organize the First National Bank, first located in Sullivan's Santa Rosa Hotel on the corner of Government and Jefferson streets, site of the Pensacola Opera House. When builder Alexander V. Clubbs completes the Opera House in 1883, the First National moves into elegant offices and parlors.

In 1892, the Merchants Bank of Pensacola purchases the First National and merges holdings as the First National Bank of Pensacola.

Brent continues to build his F. C. Brent and Company, a state bank with growing capital, and the prudent banker purchases the First National Bank in 1892. With Chipley, J. S. Leonard, W. A. Blount, W. H. Knowles, and Daniel G. Brent as directors, and acquiring Palafox Street properties north of the Customs House, the bank's new facilities at 307 South Palafox Street is described by the *The Daily News* as "the most elegant and convenient banking house and the strongest and safest bank of any city in the South."

But there were competitors—Citizens National Bank in 1892, led by President L. Hilton-Green, lumberman Rix M. Robinson, lawyer William Fisher, Adolf Greenhut of the Lewis Bear Com-

Rafters guided the logs downstream onto lures and into holds of ships. It was difficult and dangerous work.
Pensacola Historical Society

This classic photograph shows hewn timber being loaded into the specially cut holes in the hold for the transport of timber.
Pensacola Historical Society

Clara Barkley Vienne married Ebenezer Walker Dorr in 1849 and they lived in Bagdad where he was associated with E. E. Simpson Lumber Company. After Ebenezer's death in 1873, Clara built a house on Seville Square that is still preserved as a historic house museum.
Pensacola Historical Society

Anita (right) and Sally (left) were the daughters of Ebenezer and Clara Dorr.
Historic Pensacola Preservation Board

pany, and fishing company leaders Thomas E. Welles and E. E. Saunders; and American National of Pensacola, first located in the Pensacola Opera House in 1900. Within three years, American National attracts more than $600,000 in deposits, purchases the Clubbs Building at the corner of Palafox and Government streets and constructs the 1909 ten-story building, tallest in the state at the time. Later home for Florida National Bank, the renovated building shadowing Plaza Ferdinand VII is known in the 1980s as Seville Tower.

James Simpson Reese, who learns banking at First National, organizes the Peoples Bank in 1904, and turns the state-chartered institution into Peoples National Bank four years later. In 1911 the Reese banking group and the Hilton-Green-led Citizens National group form the Citizens and Peoples National Bank, which in 1918 expands into the then-vacant First National Bank Building at 215 South Palafox Street. After operating thirty-five years, First National had closed its doors in 1914, forfeiting its $500,000 investment in the devastating bankruptcy of the English timber firm of Crow, Rudolf and Company in Liverpool.

Even though Navy Yard surgeon Isaac Hulse, Dr. Robert Bell Smith Hargis, and James S. Herron pioneer Pensacola medicine and battle the dreaded yellow fever, the city lacks a civilian hospital until a temporary clinic for sick and homeless merchant seamen opens at Palafox and Romana streets during the 1867 yellow fever epidemic. Dr. Hargis, U.S. Marine Hospital surgeon who began operating a private infirmary in 1854, reestablishes the facility in New Town in 1868. Dr. Herron operates his own hospital in the old William Panton house near the corner of Barcelona and Main streets, complete with tunnel to the water's edge for passage of seamen from their vessels. Hargis and his son, Dr. Robert W. Hargis, operate the Pensacola Infirmary, destroyed by fire in 1884 and rebuilt at the Bayou Chico cantonment in 1888. For thirty-five years, Dr. Hargis dominates the proprietary hospital field; he establishes the Pensacola Medical Society, serving as its first president in 1885-1891; in 1882 he serves as president of the Florida Medical Association. County physicians Dr. Frank G. Renshaw, Dr. Warren E. Anderson and F. Elizabeth Crowell pioneer the Pensacola Infirmary, St. Anthony's Hospital, and the Pensacola Sanitarium, forerunners of the 125-bed, $480,000 Pensacola Hospital, built on Twelfth

Avenue at Gonzalez Street in 1915. Operated by the Sisters of Charity of St. Vincent de Paul, and renamed Sacred Heart in 1948, the hospital in 1965 moves into a modern North Ninth Avenue facility and develops Children's Hospital.

A Chicago-trained nurse, Elizabeth Crowell shows the emergence of women in the field, serving as hospital superintendent and stockholder. And Modeste Hargis, daughter of Dr. Robert Bell Smith Hargis, is Florida's first woman pharmacist.

With Northern lumbering declining, operators such as Michiganers George W. and Rix Robinson, New Yorker Emory Fiske Skinner, and California-born, Italian-reared William S. and Albert T. Rosasco join others in developing fifty sawmills and milltowns like Bay Point, Escambia, Century, Molino, Bluff Springs, Millview, Muscogee, and Port Washington—each, at different periods, attracting thousands of black and white workers. George Robinson with a sawmill on Pensacola Bay becomes the "King Lumberman of West Florida;" Skinner moves his operations from the Midwest, buying the Escambia Mills in 1874 and eventually acquiring 100,000 acres of timberland. By the 1880s, the Rosasco Brothers establish a thriving mill and export business from Bay Point on the Garcon peninsula.

Pensacola's leading lumber families—Baars, Keysers, Sullivans, Wrights, Yonges, Brents, Dunwodys, McLanes, and Simpsons—help shape the new prosperity by amassing substantial wealth. In addition, at Arcadia and Bagdad, timber pioneers Joseph Forsyth, Henry Hyer, and E. E. Simpson pioneer the large-scale integrated corporations flourishing in the Pensacola Bay area by the 1880s.

Absorbing the Muscogee Lumber Company in 1889, the Southern States Land and Timber Company operates three large sawmills, a dry kiln, large planing mill, lath mill, shingle mills, seventy miles of railroad, several farms and 400,000 acres of land. By 1889, with Philip Keyes Yonge manager, the company—now Southern States Lumber—annually cuts and exports thirty million feet of rough and finished lumber, and operates Magnolia Farms, a ranch with eight hundred head of cattle on its cut-over land.

Wealthy millman Gen. Russell A. Alger, former Union Army commander, Michigan governor, and secretary of war under President William McKinley, joins Northern industrialist Martin

Henry Baars brought his timber
export firm to Pensacola in
1871. He married Mary Ellison
Dunwoody. The Baars descendants
have been prominent in business and
civic affairs in the twentieth century.
Bliss Quarterly *from John Appleyard
Agency*

A. M. Moses operated a naval stores
company processing resin into
turpentine.
Bliss Quarterly *from the John
Appleyard Agency*

Sawmill scene from the 1930s era.
*John C. Pace Library, University of
West Florida*

Sullivan and Detroit business executive Edward A. Hauss to organize the Alger-Sullivan Lumber Company in northern Escambia County. They rapidly transform a settlement known as Teaspoon into Century, a milltown heralding the new century.

Acquiring large tracts of Escambia and South Alabama land, Alger-Sullivan introduces the first wide-spread reforestation. In 1939 the company sells portions of its timberland for the emergence of the new paper-making industry, led by Florida Pulp and Paper Company at Cantonment—later St. Regis; finally, in the 1980s, Champion International. In 1957, sawmiller Leon Clancy acquires Alger-Sullilvan; and his son-in-law, Warren Briggs, later Escambia County legislator and Pensacola mayor, manages the Century lumbering operation during a transformation to new corporate ownerships that produce other wood products in the last decades of the twentieth century. Alger-Sullivan, which built Century its first school, is the last Escambia timber giant, lingering long after most West Florida lumbering operations had ceased after the peak year of Pensacola port shipping in 1913.

The new Florida Constitution of 1868 establishes a state-wide system for public education, and Superintendent A. J. Pikard in 1870 operates six county schools for three months of instruction. E. E. McConnin begins classes for the first boys' high school in a rented room off Seville Square, and Sallie Ditmars opens the "Intermediate School" in her East Intendencia Street home. Except for a few Pensacola buildings, the early Escambia schools are one-room, one-teacher operations. The first major buildings, School No. 1, is built on East Wright Street.

Education pioneers Superintendent Nathan Burrell Cook, School Board members A. V. Clubbs, Philip Keyes Yonge, and George S. Hallmark, attorney and State Senator W. A. Blount, scholar Joseph Byrne Lockey, and rural teachers Annie Mae McMillian and James M. Tate help develop a system that in 1896 includes more than forty-two hundred pupils with ninety teachers earning between $27.50 and $60.00 a month.

As the century turns, Senator Blount leads the Florida legislature to authorize free schooling for twelve consecutive months, an eight-month school term and state education funding. The comprehensive system prompts construction of

more than a dozen Escambia schools, including white Pensacola High School and black Booker T. Washington High School. More than sixty teachers serve schools before World War I.

Among private academies, Henry Clay Armstrong's Pensacola Classical School represents turn-of-the-century comprehensive studies from the primary level to college preparatory courses. Armstrong's rigorous standards and liaison with Southern colleges make the classical curriculum a popular choice for North Hill families.

Known as "The Professor," Armstrong heeds Pensacolians' desire to improve local schooling for cultured citizens with his co-educational school, which he operates until retirement in 1940. The native of Macon County, Alabama, Spanish-American War veteran and 1887 civil engineer graduate of Albama Polytechnic Institute emerges as an influential Pensacolian, especially for publishing the first comprehensive history of Escambia County and inspiring reform of city government. Elected city councilman under the revised charter in 1931, Armstrong serves as mayor until 1936, and helps recruit George Rourke as the first city manager under the council form of government. The highly respected professor, known for his friendly Southern qualities, continues as a private tutor until his death in 1950.

When Geronimo, fierce, unrelenting Apache warrior of the Southwestern plains, surrenders to the U.S. Army in 1886, Pensacola businessmen Sewell C. Cobb and William and Louis Knowles see the imprisoned tribal leader as a bonanza tourist attraction for Fort Pickens. Reluctantly recognizing surrender terms that the Apaches would face no harm, the Grover Cleveland administration wants to execute Geronimo and his followers. But the Pensacolians' petition provides an alternative. Army officials had promised the Apaches they would join families already imprisoned at Castillo de San Marcos at St. Augustine. The Pensacolians argue it will be unsafe to crowd all of the Apaches in the St. Augustine fort. Cleveland orders the train carrying the Indians to deliver the seven males to Pensacola and the seventeen women, children and two scouts to St. Augustine.

Crowds circle Union Depot and line the Tarragona Street tracks as Geronimo and his band arrive in the early morning hours of October 25, 1886, and go aboard the steamer *Twin* for their island prison. Pensacolians' fears of

*Photograph of a West Florida lumber
mill taken by George Turton.
Pensacola Historical Society*

*Pensacola harbor, circa 1906.
Pensacola Historical Society*

*Palafox wharf visitors at the
E. E. Saunders Company, circa
1910.
Pensacola Historical Society*

*Warren Fish Company, 1916.
Pensacola Historical Society*

the Apaches mellow into excitement for the city's national attraction; soon trains from New Orleans and other Southern cities jammed with excursionists and yachts—including the Rockefeller family's *Alva* and the Duke of Sutherland's *Sans Pier*—enliven the city. Pensacola's first major business convention of the National Shipping League focuses additional attention on the prisoners of war.

While the national press bemoans the Apaches' "lingering death" in Florida, Geronimo entertains a continuing parade of Pickens visitors— many bringing him cigars. One of Geronimo's three wives, Ga-ah, dies and is buried in Barrancas National Cemetery. A reporter describes Geronimo's "bad Indian face—the picture of diabolical impassiveness. There is a cold glitter in his eyes, and his mouth, cut straight across his face, is hard and pitiless." But in 1888, in the middle of the night, the Army spirits the Apaches from Fort Pickens to Mount Vernon, Alabama, before Pensacolians realize the loss of their first celebrated tourist attraction. Thereafter, with Geronimo and the Apaches prisoners of war for twenty-five years, Pensacolians feed the legend; they erect historical markers and designate a "Geronimo cell" for Pickens visitors.

Republican leaders Sewell Cobb, Emory Fiske Skinner, and John M. Tarble find their party fading as Pensacola's county political leaders shift allegiance to the Democrats in the mid-1880s.

Political rhetoric swirls around the Mullets, led by Stephen Mallory II, son of the Confederate navy secretary who serves in the Florida House in 1876 and Florida Senate from 1880-1890, and Colonel Chipley's blue-stocking Snappers. It's the middle class versus disciples of Chipley's Tammany Association.

In the 1870s, Irish-born Pensacola lawyer Charles W. Jones, formerly of Bluff Springs, rises from his trade as Santa Rosa County carpenter to complete law studies and discover politics. Defeated for Congress in 1872, Jones goes to the U.S. Senate as the first Democrat from Florida three years later. Jones' victory symbolizes the decline of Reconstruction Republicanism. And Mallory and other county leaders help re-elect Jones in 1882. The skillful young senator attracts national attention and is hinted for attorney general in the Grover Cleveland administration.

Jones represents Florida from 1875 until 1887—re-elected without campaigning in 1882—but a nervous collapse, erratic behavior and infatuation with a wealthy Detroit woman lead the Jones family to have the senator committed to a Dearborn, Michigan Catholic mental institution in 1890. Never recovering, Jones dies in 1897.

Gen. Edward A. Perry, Democratic activist, defeats Republican-endorsed Frank Pope for governor in 1884, and his narrow victory at home reflects the brewing power struggle between his friend, Colonel Chipley, and Mallory's Mullets. Perry appoints Chipley city commissioner after ratification of the 1885 Constitution allows the governor to replace the post-Reconstruction "black and tan" municipal government with an all-white provisional commission. Chipley becomes mayor, and Mallory's Mullets openly accuse Perry of representing big business. The appointed commission aggressively seeks to strengthen the city's financial position, remove it from corrupt political influences, bring law and order to downtown and disenfranchise blacks.

Resistance to Chipley builds, especially from Editor J. Dennis Wolfe of the *Pensacola Commercial,* who accuses the railroader of deception and implies scandal. Wolfe writes: "Look here, Major Octopus, you can't talk politics, run the state of Florida, do a general land office business and run the railroad at the same time. Your tentacles will get tangled and suckers exhausted by too much labor." He labels Chipley "Governor Chipley," finally reducing his name to "little octopus." Chipley retaliates: "I with the utmost deliberation and premeditation denounce him as a willful and malicious liar and libeler and I apply the brand trusting that it may sink in his debased soul deep enough to touch his manhood . . . let the liar wear the brand if there remains space under his tattooed body to hear his last violation of truth, justice, and decency."

Wolfe, a former Union officer from Monmouth, Illinois, who commanded black Union occupation troops in Pensacola, emerges from a controversial law practice during Reconstruction with a poisonous newspaper pen. Shot at more than once, the *Commercial* editor carries a loaded Navy Colt by his side while traveling by buggy on Pensacola streets. Barred from practicing law in Judge William Kirk's county court, Wolfe is drawn into a Palafox and Intendencia street shootout with the angered judge on September 6, 1869. Kirk, former editor of the radical Republican *Tri-Weekly Observer,* the only Pensacola newspaper to survive the Civil War, draws his pistol and fires at Wolfe; both men empty their revolvers before Wolfe scrambles inside a store operated by Jasper and Viola Gonzalez. Using Raymond Knowles' gun, Kirk keeps firing; Wolfe retreats on Palafox Street. None of the gunshots hit either man, but Kirk meets Wolfe again—in the courtroom. The jury clears Wolfe; Kirk is eventually disbarred.

Kirk's *Observer,* launched with Frank Touart and M. F. Gonzalez and pledging allegiance to the Union during the occupation, vanishes when Touart and Gonzalez begin a new newspaper era with the *Tri-Weekly West Florida Commercial.* In 1888, the *Commercial,* a Democratic newspaper edited by Wolfe, becomes the *Pensacola Daily Commercial,* deeming itself "the only live newspaper in this city" with a colorful harbor scene decorating its nameplate. Its competitor, *The Pensacolian,* founded in 1883 by Benjamin Robinson and John O'Connor, and equally Democratic, emphasizes literary content of magazine quality.

Constant attacks by Wolfe's *Commercial*—coupled with Chipley's political aspirations, and the bitter Snapper-Mullet feud—lead John O'Connor, founder of *The Pensacolian,* and John C. Witt to approach Pensacola businessman in January 1889 for $10,000 backing for a new morning newspaper. They form the News Publishing Company with Hugh B. Hatton, president; William Fisher, vice president; Richard M. Cary, Jr., secretary; Thomas C. Watson, treasurer; and W. H. Knowles, J. T. Whiting, W. A. D'Alemberte, E. E. Saunders, W. B. Wright, and F. G. Renshaw, directors. O'Connor is managing editor and Witt is business manager.

The News, a four-page, $5-a-year newspaper produced by a ten-person staff in the Armory Hall at the corner of Palafox and Intendencia streets, supports Chipley's Tammany Association and his ambitions to unseat U.S. Senator Wilkinson Call. *The News* views Chipley's 1895 election to the Florida senate as a significant victory over the Call-Mallory coalition—and then pushes for his selection as U.S. senator. Chipley and Mallory are drawn into a tense, emotional, and complex Tallahassee caucus to unseat Call. Yet Chipley's campaign is shattered by Mallory, chosen for the Senate seat in the bitter, lengthy battle on the twenty-fifth ballot.

Returning to Pensacola, Chipley is hailed as a conquering hero. The Chipley Light Infantry fires six volleys as the colonel's railroad car reaches Union Depot, and a cheering crowd hears the defeated candidate say, "I have no criticism of Mr. Mallory . . . My prime objective was to retire from political life Wilkinson Call. This I accomplished."

Yet Chipley's time is short. On December 1, 1897, the year Stephen R. Mallory enters the U.S. Senate, William Dudley Chipley dies suddenly in Washington, D.C., at age fifty-seven.

Chipley is buried in his native Columbus, although Pensacolians wanted the railroad-builder interred in their city. In tribute, Pensacolians erect the granite monument in Plaza Ferdinand VII, heralding him "Soldier-Statesman-Benefactor . . . The history of his life is the history of the up-building of West Florida, and its every material advancement, for two decades, bears the impress of his genius and his labor."

Ironically, Wolfe dies the same year as Chipley. The editor's daughter, Agnes, is a pioneer Escambia County educator for whom Agnes McReynolds school is named.

In July 1898, Manager and Editor Frank L. Mayes converts William M. Lofton's one-year-old weekly *Pensacola Journal* into a daily competitor to *The Daily News.* A twenty-three-year-old printer editor from the South Dakota frontier, Mayes operates a Democratic newspaper reflecting Southern Progressivism on the dawn of the twentieth century.

Pensacolians perceive Mayes as a brave and independent editor who calls the aldermanic form of city government cumbersome; he campaigns for a city commission and helps write the new city charter approved by voters in 1913. Mayes supports women's suffrage, opposes the convict-lease system and fee system then prevalent in West Florida, and advocates government ownership of all public service—railroads, telephone, and telegraph. Protesting corruption in city government, Mayes considers West Florida controlled by the L & N Railroad, and wages a continual battle against its influences and practices. The *Journal* advocates a city-owned dock complex—approved by city voters—but not fulfilled in Mayes' lifetime. A persistent advocate for educational reform, Mayes seeks to educate readers and chides *The Daily News* and old-line Pensacolians for lack of progressive thinking. His editorials urge penal reform, rehabilitation rather than punishment for juvenile and adult offenders, abolishing the death penalty, eco-

Fishermen bringing in the catch.
Pensacola Historical Society

Sailors with some of their ship repair tools.
Pensacola Historical Society

Red Snappers being unloaded on Pensacola bayfront..
Pensacola Historical Society

Ice being loaded on the fishing boats.
Pensacola Historical Society

Pensacola fishing boats make the city
the "Red Snapper capital of the world."
Pensacola Historical Society

Dr. J. S. Herron's residence, Palafox and Jackson streets was built around 1880. The three-story house had about ten thousand square feet of space. The closet doors on the upper floor lifted vertically into the attic. Dr. Herron was an early history buff who wrote a history of Pensacola for a 1909 newspaper article. The house was used by the Knights of Columbus after 1924. It was razed in 1963.
Pensacola Historical Society

The Albert Riera house on Belmont Street in North Hill at the turn of the century.
Pensacola Historical Society

The Watson house on Gregory Street, early 1900s.
Pensacola Historical Society

nomic development, regulation of big business, city beautification, better health education, prohibition, and improvement of cultural activities.

Florida newspapers champion Mayes for governor or congress, but the *Journal* editor-owner refuses all political patronage except that of Customs Collector for the Port of Pensacola. As a conservationist Mayes cites esthetics in his campaign for removal of the city's dilapidated fences; he convinces the L&N Railroad to spend $20,000 for the 17th Avenue underpass as part of his crusade to pave a highway around Bayou Texar and build better roads and highways as stimulant for tourism.

Mayes' *Journal* looks to the new century, declaring "Pensacola's Watchwords, Boost, Boom and Build—That's All." He calls for the "Atlanta Spirit," exhorting Pensacolians to "wake up and work for the Deep Water City." He blames opponents of progress as the real enemies, editorializing, "Wanted—a Few First Class funerals in Pensacola." He claims "dead ones"—by keeping their money in vaults and socks—still make Pensacola decisions, and if all defenders of "Old Pensacola" were really to die at once, the city could afford to erect a monument for them or at least a historical marker. Mayes calls for boosting Pensacola as the best Gulf Coast port, natural terminus of northern railways, and the center of a fertile and prolific agricultural region. He develops a creed for leading the Deep Water City to the "highest rank of Southern municipalities."

Mayes' premature death in 1915 saddens Pensacolians. Mardi Gras and the tenth anniversary celebration of Hotel San Carlos are postponed because of his death. National figures pay tribute to his leadership—among them his personal friend, Josephus Daniels, secretary of the Navy, who writes, "There is not an editor in all the South whom I was most sincerely attached. My

Unidentified residence of a middle class turn-of-the-century black family.
Pensacola Historical Society

The congregation of the Norwegian Seaman's Church is seen here at Christmas circa 1895. This building on South Palafox was destroyed in 1934.
Pensacola Historical Society

This is Temple Beth-el on East Chase Street circa 1900. The first synogogue in Florida was built in 1876 by the Temple Beth-el congregation. Fire destroyed the two buildings. The synogogue is now located on Palafox and Cervantes.
Pensacola Historical Society

attachment was born in recognition of his unselfish devotion to those principles which he believed would do most to promote the common weal."

Two devastating fires, in 1880 and 1905, shatter Pensacola's business district, but by 1910 a new skyline emerges with The U.S. Custom House, Court House, Opera House, Pensacola Athletic Club, Thiesen Building, Brent Building, Blount Building, Jefferson Street City Hall and Hotel San Carlos. Chipley and A.V. Clubbs had recognized Plaza Ferdinand for its beauty and historical significance, and in the New Century the park had iron railings, planted trees and sidewalks.

But with repeated and devastating hurricane damage, and the long scar of denuded West Florida forests, Pensacolians find their timber bonanza ending by 1910. Foreign port trade dwindles, and financial disasters signal the long economic depression leading to World War I. And Pensacolians, again banking their hopes on the U.S. Navy, are unsure of the fate to the diminishing old Navy Yard mission.

A St. Joseph's Catholic Church School graduating class poses in the late 1920s.
Pensacola Historical Society

The original First Presbyterian Church was occupied in 1848 on Intendencia Street.
Pensacola Historical Society

In 1889 the Presbyterians built a new church on Chase Street that served the congregation until 1968 when they moved to the sanctuary on Gregory Street.
Pensacola Historical Society

The First Baptist Church, seen here in 1906, was completed in 1895 and remodeled in 1922 and 1956.
Pensacola Historical Society

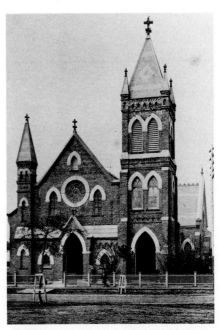

Christ Episcopal Church congregation moved in 1903 to the current building at Wright and Palafox.
Pensacola Historical Society

St. Michael's Catholic Church, built in 1886, and seen here as it appeared in the early 1900s, is located at Palafox and Chase streets.
Pensacola Historical Society

Interior of the Greek Orthodox
Church on East Garden circa 1930.
Pensacola Historical Society

The Liollio family is one of the early
Greek immigrant families that came to
Pensacola after the Civil War. Left to
right are Angelo D. Liollio,
Constantine A. Apostle, Paul D.
Liollio, and Constantine D. Apollo.
Pensacola Historical Society

The East Hill Trolley in the early
1900s is stopped in front of the
present-day courthouse.
Pensacola Historical Society

Kupfrian's Park circa 1885 was a
favorite picnic and fun area.
Pensacola Historical Society

Gulf Power plant circa 1930s.
Gulf Power Archives

Gulf Power Station on October 8, 1906.
Gulf Power Archives

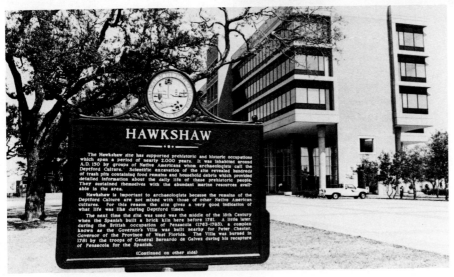

The new Gulf Power corporate headquarters on Bayfront Parkway is built in an area known as Hawkshaw. Prior to construction, a Deptford Indian village and several historic sites were uncovered in an excavation funded by Gulf Power. Artifacts from the archaeological project are exhibited in the building and several books were published on interpretation of the site and the artifacts that were recovered.
Gulf Power Archives

Francis C. Brent was the founder of the First National Bank and developer of the Brent Block in downtown Pensacola.
Pensacola Historical Society

Thomas C. Watson was a real estate agent, First Mutual founder, and a Pensacola promoter.
Pensacola Historical Society

Knowles Brothers Insurance and Real Estate office.
Pensacola Historical Society

Brent Brothers Grocery Store on Palafox in the 1870s.
Pensacola Historical Society

Brent family at Christmas circa 1905.
Pensacola Historical Society

The Brent and Watson families posed circa 1910. Standing left to right are George Brent, William Brent, Mollie Brent, Robert Brent, Genevieve Brent Turtle, Jim Watson, Cora Brent Warren, Tina Brent, and Rufus Manley. Sitting left to right are Mollie Brent Mare, Thomas Brent, Belle Brent, T. C. Brent, Catherine Brent Watson and Celeste Brent Manley. Children left to right in front are Brent Watson, Tommy Watson, and Frances Louise Brent.
Pensacola Historical Society

J. M. Hilliard Carriage Shop on Garden Street circa 1880s.
Pensacola Historical Society

First Mutual Savings and Loan moved into its new building on Baylen Street in 1960. First Mutual joined the AmSouth Bancorporation of Birmingham in 1987 and celebrates its one-hundredth anniversary in 1989.
Pensacola News-Journal *Files*

A. V. Clubbs was a prominent citizen, contractor, and influential School Board member for whom A. C. Clubbs School was named.
Pensacola Historical Society

First National Bank interior circa 1899. The bank was located at 307 South Palafox from 1893 to 1908 and moved to its new location at 215 South Palafox in 1908. That building became the home of the Citizens and Peoples Bank in 1918.
Pensacola Historical Society

The Pensacola Opera House was built in 1893. Damaged by the 1916 hurricane, it was destroyed by a ferocious storm in 1917. Elements of the building were used for building the Saenger Theatre.
Pensacola Historical Society

These couples from a Floradora production in the Opera House are, left to right, Mamie Merritt and J. C. Watson, Bertie White and Willie Howe, and Daisy Howe and W. M. McClellan.
Pensacola Historical Society

W. A. Blount, city attorney, member of the 1885 and 1892 state constitutional conventions and state senator, married Cora Nellie Moreno and fathered seven children.
Pensacola Historical Society

Mrs. Clara Garnier Dorr Blount was the wife of A. C. Blount, Sr., and the daughter of the Dorr family of Bagdad.
Historic Pensacola Preservation Board

U.S. Customs and Post Office building, 1874, from a stereoscope card.
Pensacola Historical Society

Ten Story American National Bank of Pensacola
The highest Building in Florida. Erected at a cost of $250,000.
Fire-Proof in construction. Pensacola, Fla.

Rix M. Robinson, founder and operator of a major lumber mill, was also Pensacola postmaster.
John Appleyard Agency photo

The American National Bank, constructed 1909, was the tallest building in Florida when constructed. It is now Seville Tower office building.
Pensacola Historical Society

The Citizens and Peoples Bank, seen here circa 1951, is located at 215 South Palafox. It was formerly First National.
Pensacola Historical Society

Modeste Hargis (1875-1948) was the first licensed female pharmacist in the state of Florida in the 1890s. She was the daughter of Robert B. S. Hargis, who founded the Pensacola Medical Society in 1873.
Pensacola Historical Society

Francis Elizabeth Crowell, pictured here circa 1900, practiced her profession as a nurse in Pensacola from 1896 to 1905. She served as superintendent of St. Anthony's Hospital and Sanitorium Training School for Nurses in Pensacola and was also a major stockholder in that corporation. She made significant contributions to the nursing profession after she left Pensacola.
Pensacola Historical Society

This is Pensacola Hospital in the early 1900s. It later became Sacred Heart Hospital then the Pensacola School of Liberal Arts. It is now an office building.
Pensacola Historical Society

Hargis Pharmacy interior, circa 1900.
Pensacola Historical Society

Emory Fiske Skinner, who wrote his
Reminiscenses in 1908, operated a
major lumber company on Escambia
Bay.
Reminiscenses by E. F. Skinner

The Rosasco family had a prosperous
international shipping business. Their
homestead was at Bay Point on the Gar-
con Peninsula in Santa Rosa County.
Seated, Dick Rosasco and Walter,
3; Mrs. Rosasco and baby Adrian;
Adelia, 7; standing, Aunt Jane
Jackson, Uncle Manuel and Norman
Garrett.
Historic Pensacola Preservation Board

Cottage Hill Store and Post Office in North Escambia, circa 1910-1920. Florida State University photo

P. K. Yonge served on the Board of Education for fifteen years in the 1880s and 1890s. His personal collection of manuscripts form the core of the special collections at the University of Florida P. K. Yonge library in Gainesville.
Pensacola Historical Society

This unidentified farm in Escambia County may be Magnolia Farms.
Pensacola Historical Society

*Unidentified ladies making butter in
the 1920s.
Pensacola Historical Society*

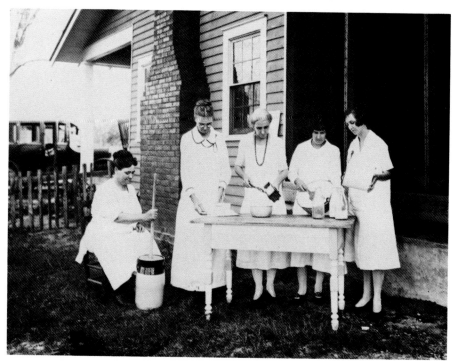

*Public School No. 1 on East Wright
Street circa 1890.
Pensacola Historical Society*

*Annie McMillan is the teacher at right
with this school group circa 1909.
Pensacola Historical Society*

Judge E. Dixie Beggs came to Pensacola in 1896 and served as judge from 1896 to 1913. He married Lily Clubbs, daughter of A. V. Clubbs, and was active with the school board. His son, E. Dixie Beggs, was one of two Pensacola lawyers to serve as president of the Florida State Bar Association. Pensacola Historical Society

Mrs. Annie K. Suter, a dedicated school teacher, was later honored when a school was named for her. Pensacola Historical Society

Occie Clubbs, daughter of A. V. Clubbs, became a school teacher and principal, and was active as writer and historian and Pensacola Historical Society leader.
Historic Pensacola Preservation Board

J. M. Tate began teaching at Ferry Pass School in 1879. The James M. Tate Agricultural School near Gonzalez gave education and support for the agricultural growth in northern Escambia county.
Pensacola Historical Society

Elementary School No. 3, students with their teacher, Minnie Gaskins
Pensacola Historical Society

Pensacola High School, 1921-1952, adjacent to Lee Square. This photo was taken during the 1940s; it was destroyed by fire in 1959.
Pensacola Historical Society

Pensacola High School, Class Day 1922.
Pensacola Historical Society

Miss Pensacola circa 1922. The inscription on the cup reads: "Atlantic City Pageant Rolling Chair Parade."
Pensacola Historical Society

Adult Education class at Washington
High School, 1935.
Florida State University photo

Professor H. Clay Armstrong and his
wife Janet opened the Pensacola Classi-
cal School in 1900. The popular private
institution that gave instruction from
primary to college level. Armstrong
(left) is seen here (1934) presenting
a key to the city as a kickoff for an
American Red Cross celebration.
Pensacola Historical Society

Pensacola Classical School's basketball team. Back row, left to right are Willis, Leonard, D'Alemberte, Professor Armstrong; others unidentified. Front row, are Wells, Harvey, Quina, Oerting, and Hagerman.
Pensacola Historical Society

Apache prisoners of war, at Fort Pickens from 1886 to 1888, were Pensacola's first tourist attractions. Among them were the famed Geronimo, left; Chief Naiche, middle; and Chief Mangus, right.
Pensacola Historical Society

Frank L. Mayes, editor of the Journal from 1900 to 1915, sought to improve the community through editorials urging education, regulation of public utilities, and other business and governmental reform.
Pensacola Historical Society

The Pensacola News-Journal *built its new building on Romana Street in 1949 and remodeled it in 1977 adding bricks from the Old Spanish Trail to form the sidewalks and plaza as a historical memorial.*
Pensacola News-Journal *Files*

The Pensacola Daily News *was the forerunner of today's Pensacola News-Journal. The year 1989 marks the one-hundredth anniversary of the daily newspaper in Pensacola.*
Pensacola Historical Society

Pensacola News-Journal *publisher Braden Ball gave annual barbecues in the 1960s and 1970s. Thousands of well-known politicians, journalists, and civic leaders gathered at his Woodbine Springs farm, in Santa Rosa County.*
Pensacola News-Journal *Files*

Marion T. Gaines, (left) editor of the Pensacola News-Journal *from 1939 to 1965; A. C. Blount, (middle) First Mutual Savings and Loan officer and civic leader; and Braden Ball, (right), president and publisher of the Pensa-cola News-Journal *from 1942 to 1976.* Pensacola News-Journal *Files*

Maurice F. (Moose) Harling, govern-mental writer and editor for the Pensacola News-Journal *from 1945 to 1970. He was the only Florida newspaperman ever honored by both houses of the Florida legislature.* Pensacola News-Journal *Files*

Pat Lloyd was a News-Journal *writer for forty-one years. She covered all topics from fashion to politics but was probably best known for the Tony Knight column, a potpourri of politics, social items, and "chit chat." Here she is receiving recognition from the Flor-ida Public Relations Association in January 1987. She died of cancer later that year.* Pensacola News-Journal *Files*

The tugboat E. E. Simpson aground at the L & N Railroad wharf after the 1906 Hurricane.
Pensacola Historical Society

The 1926 Hurricane did a lot of damage to Pensacola wharves. The Mineola is surrounded by debris in the foreground.
Pensacola Historical Society

The Oerting family operated a ship chandler's business from 1862 for more than one hundred years. Seated at left is Peter Julius Oerting, ninety-four; seated at right is Charlie McKenzie Oerting, sixty; standing are Charles Julius Oerting, Sr., forty; and Charles Julius Oerting, Jr., twelve.
Historic Pensacola Preservation Board

The McKenzie-Oerting's ship chandler's store operated from the late 1860s to the 1970s. The South Palafox Street structure remains one of the bayfront historical landmarks.
Pensacola Historical Society

Interior of the Parlor Meat Market located on S. Palafox.
Pensacola Historical Society

*Manuel G. Largue horseshoeing circa
1890s.
Pensacola Historical Society*

*The Broadbent and Durham families
posed in front of the U.S. Life Saving
Station on Santa Rosa Island circa
1900-1910. Captain Broadbent, back
row middle, was the superintendent of
the station.
Pensacola Historical Society*

*Lighthouse and keeper's quarters lo-
cated near Fort Barrancas, circa 1880.
Pensacola Historical Society*

Mr. Whiting, lighthouse keeper, circa 1916.
Pensacola Historical Society

"Just Fishing." Identified are Julia Lloyd Lee, standing second from right; Stephen Lee, sitting far right; William F. Lee, Jr., sitting far left; Margaret McClay, seated third from right.
Pensacola Historical Society

Sacarro's Bathhouse at the turn of the century was located off shore near South Florida Blanca Street.
Pensacola Historical Society

Bathers circa 1900, at Pensacola Beach.
Delores Pittman photo

Pensacola Yacht Club headquarters in the early 1920s was aboard the General Wilson, a concrete boat built during World War I and berthed in Bayou Chico.
Pensacola Historical Society

Swimmers at Bayview Park circa 1900.
Pensacola Historical Society

These turn of the century bathers are seen at Pensacola Beach.
Pensacola Historical Society

The 1902 Mardi Gras Court inside
the Opera house. Left to right stand-
ing are A. Brooks, Agnes Casey,
Campbell Avery, Annie Baars, King
Major R. M. Carey, Buckner Chipley,
Queen Daisy Wright, Celestine Brent,
Knowles Hyer, Daisy Hyer, Dick
Turner, and C. E. Merritt.
Pensacola Historical Society

Pensacola's baseball team, the Dudes,
in the 1890s.
Pensacola Historical Society

The Tarpon *ferried visitors to Santa Rosa Island and the Gulf Breeze Peninsula for picnics, camping, and other excursions. A well-known expression of Captain Willis Green Barrow, the skipper, was "God makes the weather, but I make the trips." The Tarpon sank in 1937 carrying Barrow and his crew to their deaths.*
Pensacola Historical Society

The Pensacola Athletic Club, early 1900s. Top row, left to right, are Martinez, Liddon, Unger, Manager Schad, and Shuttleworth, and unidentified. Middle row are Oerting, Thiegson, Kinsley, Wells, Richards. Front row are Quina, Baars, Quina, Touart.
Pensacola Historical Society

Pensacola Vocal Society in 1915. Photo taken from program for the thirty-first annual session of the Florida Chautauqua at DeFuniak Springs.
Florida State University photo

Carnival on West Chase Street. Delores Pittman photo

Magnolia Bluff on Escambia Bay was a popular camping area reached by train in the mid-1880s.
Pensacola Historical Society

Commissary tent at a camp set up by the U.S. Naval Drill group at the Magnolia Bluff area during the Spanish-American War.
Pensacola Historical Society

Saltmarsh summer camp along Scenic Highway circa 1900.
Pensacola Historical Society

One of the twelve-inch disappearing guns installed in Battery Pensacola in Fort Pickens prior to World War I circa 1908-1909.
Gulf Islands National Seashore

Civil War Confederate Veterans organization, circa 1919, in front of the Armory Building that was next door to the old Escambia County Courthouse on North Palafox.
Photo courtesy of Toni Moore Clevenger

The 1918 Liberty Loan Drive
Parade at Palafox and Garden.
Pensacola Historical Society

Emma Chandler, well-known Pensacola artist, moved to Pensacola from
Tennessee, studied art in New York,
and opened an art institute in Pensacola in the 1880s.
Pensacola Historical Society

Manuel Runyan, artist and teacher, historical buff, and occasional music teacher, studied under Emma Chandler and actively painted from the 1890s until his death in 1954.
Historic Pensacola Preservation Board

Life and Miss Celeste by Florence Palmer (circa 1937) is the title of a novel that centers on life in Pensacola at the turn of the century. The two main characters were based on two local sisters. "Miss Celeste" was Dolores Charbonier and "Miss Helene" was Pauline Charbonier.
T. T. Wentworth, Jr.

The Brosnaham family and other relatives are, in back, Mr. G. O. Brosnaham; in second row, left to right, are Mable Brosnaham; Mrs. N. C. Shakleford; and unidentified; in front row, are Dr. G. O. Brosnaham, Mrs. Tate, child; Prof. J. M. Tate; and Billy Cary. Historic Pensacola Preservation Board

The Bear sisters are, left to right, Eunice Gerson, Gladys Cahn, Hilda Bear, and Miriam Friedman. Pensacola Historical Society

These couples, left to right, are Mr.
and Mrs. John Merritt, Mr. and Mrs.
Drohman, and Mr. and Mrs. Walter
Garfield.
Pensacola Historical Society

The Merritt children are, standing left
to right, Mary Elizabeth Merritt and
Em Turner Merritt. Seated are Jack
and Doris Merritt.
Pensacola Historical Society

Jim Brown, founder of the Zion Burial Society.
Pensacola Historical Society

Pensacola Fire Department No. 3 Truck House at Zaragoza and Commendencia streets circa 1909. Left to right are Jack Matthews, Willie Bicker, Len Davis, Buck O'Connell, unidentified, and James Barry Graham.
Pensacola Historical Society

Members of the Germania Hose Company originally organized in 1870. Fires were nearly always disasters until 1886 when the water company finally succeeded in providing an adequate water supply.
Pensacola Historical Society

*Capt. James A. Daw, Pensacola Police
Force circa 1900.
Pensacola Historical Society*

*Pensacola Police Department circa
1930s in front of City Hall.
Pensacola Historical Society*

The Pensacola Draymen's Exchange dispatched draymen to deliver various types of goods to houses and stores circa 1910.
Pensacola Historical Society

A 1921 Hygeia Coca-Cola delivery truck. The company began operation about 1903.
Pensacola Historical Society

Citizens urge voters to pass legislation to
provide better roads.
Pensacola Historical Society

Ingham Dairy wagon early 1900s.
Pensacola Historical Society

Southern Bell Telephone Company
car by Plaza Ferdinand in early 1900s.
Delores Pittman photo

140

Cotton being taken to the compress in late 1920s. Some 150,000 bales of cotton were exported through Pensacola ports in 1904.
Pensacola Historical Society

A streetcar strike in 1908 brought a call by the mayor for the state militia which camped on Palafox Street until local citizens could be deputized to preserve law and order. The strike lasted thirty-eight days and finally sixteen of the strikers went back to work. It was the worst strike in Pensacola history.
Pensacola Historical Society

Two gentlemen cross Plaza Ferdinand. In the background to the right is the Opera House circa 1910-13.
Pensacola Historical Society

The 1911 Battleship Florida naval
forces parade in front of the Hotel
San Carlos.
Historic Pensacola Preservation Board

Plaza Ferdinand VII at the corner of
Palafox and Government in the mid-
1920s.
Pensacola Historical Society

Escambia County Court House and
Armory 1937. Left to right are Frank
Pause, T. C. McCoy, E. B. Creighton,
H. A. Brosnaham, J. N. Rauscher,
Langley Bell, Bernie Davis, H. E. Page,
Forsythe Caro, T. T. Wentworth, Jr.,
W. J. McDavid, J. Lawrence Mayo,
John Cole, J. L. Robins, W. B.
Strickland, Sam Roseman, J. V.
Varnum, John Lewis Reese, and C. B.
Fields.
T. T. Wentworth, Jr.

The turn-of-the-century U.S. Post Office is now the Escambia County Court House.
Pensacola Historical Society

The Continental Hotel at right was known as the Chase house in the 1870s. An 1884 addition is shown at the left. By 1892 it was known as the Escambia Hotel.
Pensacola Historical Society

The Seminole Hotel circa 1930 on Gregory Street was built by the Simpsons who owned the Bagdad Lumber Mill. Later used as a rooming house, it was demolished around 1945.
Pensacola Historical Society

Naval Aviator Walter L. Richardson, left, a ship's cook who owned his own camera, in a 1916 flight with Commander E. Johnson.
U.S. Navy photo

9

Wings of Gold

To fly, to soar; to be aloft with the earth spinning below; to climb beyond the earth's gravity into unknowns of space. These are dreams of wingless men and women for all the ages; dreams of young U.S. Navy pioneers in Pensacola with man-made wings in 1914.

They jerk skyward in strange contraptions—the aeroplane: a glorified kite tied together with wire, wood, and canvas. Sputtering gasoline-fed engines propel pilots on wobbly tests of solo courage and daring.

Then, in the 1930s and 1940s, roaring engines and whirling propellers thunder a symphony of air power in skies worldwide. In midcentury, silvery winged Navy jets slide across the high blue, echoing their inferno blasts in a searing release from their own shrill bang of cracking the sound barrier.

Across frontiers of America's air age—an evolution spanning more than three-quarters of a century—Pensacolians experience the maturity of naval flight. They have known early flying machines and seaplanes and their magnificent daredevils in open cockpits, portable tent hangars adorning the beach, primitive floating airfields attached to Navy vessels, dirigible balloons, and Navy fleets of the world in Pensacola harbor. On the dawn of the 1990s they see the future on wingtips of the Blue Angels, the

Pensacola-based navy flight demonstration team. Navy leaders describe the Angels, jetting across Pensacola skies, appearing in cities across America and in foreign lands, as the best recruiting poster ever designed and akin to the American flag in patriotic pride.

In 1986, celebrating the Navy's proven precision tool of national defense in four wars, aviation visionaries and pioneers, World War I and World War II pilots, and those of the Jet Age gather for a Pensacola homecoming. They celebrate the seventy-fifth anniversary of the birth of naval aviation. Aging men with leathery, eroded faces who wore wings of gold are drawn into star-spangled ceremony and nostalgic reunions, and entertained by comedian Bob Hope and other film and TV celebrities on Hope's NBC "75th Naval Aviation Anniversary" television show filmed aboard the training carrier USS *Lexington*. They share with the nation the honor and pride of newer generations of Navy pilots electronically paving jet avenues in Pensacola skies and continuing the legacy of the Cradle of Naval Aviation and Annapolis of the Air. They salute the many Pensacola-trained Navy astronauts who piloted an assortment of spacecraft from capsules to the *Challenger* and *Discovery* shuttles, beginning with the first American in space on May 5, 1961—Alan Bartlett Shepard, Jr.

Yet naval aviation's beginning and evolution in

Pensacola come as hidden blessings for an earlier Pensacola. Living in an old seaport with a obsolescent Navy Yard, Pensacolians are unaware a new instrument of naval warfare will soon rise skyward from their sandy harbor beaches.

With the Navy sunset near in Pensacola in the second decade of twentieth century, men of the sea sprout wings, finding an enduring nest on sandy West Florida shores.

The 1825 Navy Yard—some Pensacolians still use the reference—is eighty years old and targeted for oblivion on October 20, 1911. The old yard and adjacent U.S. Army Post of Fort Barrancas still show scars of Civil War destruction. Anger from the Gulf continues the destruction and discomfort of the lonely Navy and Army garrisons.

Six Army officers and 125 soldiers still man the harbor fortifications from the post that has been expanded with officers' quarters, Barrancas Barracks, stables, commissary, shops, storehouses, and the 1895-built hospital near the villages of Warrington and Woolsey. They maintain Barrancas National Cemetery, which had been established in 1868.

The 1906 hurricane had devastated the Pensacola area, erasing the crumbling ruins of Fort McRee on Foster's Bank and splintering the new Navy construction. Two years later, another yellow fever epidemic had further hindered new construction.

Now, with the yard closing, Pensacolians remember their struggle for military identity. The Spanish-American War in 1898 spurs Pensacolians' belief their harbor will be a natural site for troop embarkation and a base for supplies for forces operating against Cuba. Pensacolians are excited about "America's Splendid Little War." An editorial in the anxious *Daily News* is sarcastic: "Troops have not yet been sent here because we have pure and abundant water, fine camping grounds, and transportation facilities. They are not located here because it is the ideal spot for the concentration of troops where the gulf breezes and the sea-bathing is glorious." Yet the *News* reports "an immense searchlight, with an eight-foot fence" at Fort Pickens lighting the Gulf at night "bright as day for miles. There is no danger of a Spanish boat sneaking around these ports."

But on June 1, 1898, Tampa is the embarkation destination of Theodore Roosevelt's Cuba-bound Rough Riders when six trains carrying men of the First U.S. Volunteer Cavalry from Texas training camps arrive at Pensacola's Union Passenger Station. The Rough Riders delight cheering, flag-waving crowds, and Colonel Roosevelt stirs downtown onlookers by lunching at the Cordova Coffee Saloon. But after most of a day in Pensacola, they train south.

The war flurry brings long overdue repairs to the Navy Yard and a small wooden drydock, and the Barrancas Army post became headquarters for the Coast Artillery Corps defending Pensacola harbor. The big armament of the new Endicott system of coastal defense rises from new concrete batteries, partially obscuring the Civil War-damaged brick artistry of Fort Pickens on Santa Rosa Island and the ruins of Fort McRee on Foster's bank. Artillery guns mounted on disappearing-type carriages are encased in massive reinforced concrete structures and protected by thick earth embankments. Submarine mine fields guard the harbor approaches, protected by rapid-firing small caliber artillery.

But Pensacola—again ready for hostilities—remains remote from events in Cuba. Acquisition of Guantanamo Bay in Cuba further diminishes Pensacola as a naval station.

Yet the quietness of Pensacola harbor fortifications is shattered in June 1899 when fire at Fort Pickens ignites a powder magazine, ripping out a section of the brick wall, splintering nearby Army wooden buildings and propelling fragments of bricks across the bay into Warrington. The *Journal* reports Navy firefighters and a detachment of Marines "at great peril extinguish the fire, save the forts, the large powder magazine and cover themselves with glory . . . Had the larger magazine blown up there is no telling what damage would have been done there."

The gaping fort cavity is mere memory in 1911, when the decommissioning of the Navy Yard rocks the Pensacola community. Sensing an end of an era with Washington's decisions, Pensacola oldtimers lament, "It was like leaving a home never to return."

Commandant Lucien Young, who had endeared himself to the community leadership, officially closes the gates at 5:00 p.m., October 11; three days later he leaves for Key West by train. Most of the yard's stores and equipment are shipped to Key West and Charleston naval stations; the Marine guard goes to Norfolk. Only three watchmen and a small group of caretakers remain.

But elsewhere, portending Pensacola's future, the Navy Department experiments with three newly purchased flying machines. Actually, the Navy crystallizes an idea first advanced by Theodore Roosevelt, who as assistant secretary of the Navy in 1898 recommended studies for the military application of Professor Samuel P. Langley's flying machine, the Aerodome. Although the experiments fail, naval observers are still intrigued by the phenomenon.

Ten months prior to Pensacola's jarring base-closing, Lt. Theodore Gordon (Spuds) Ellyson, Naval Aviator No. 1, sputters aloft in a Glenn Hammond Curtiss' hydro-aeroplane at North Island, California, giving birth to the Navy's age of flight. Ellyson is the only U.S. naval aviator—the first ordered to train at Curtiss' California aviation camp. His mastery of the A-1, a Curtiss Model E Triad, on the shores of Cocoa Lake, Hammondsport, New York, proves the aeroplane capable of being flown from land or water by means of an innovative centerline float and retractable wheels.

Civilian pilot Eugene Ely forecasts the age of the aircraft carrier on November 11, 1910, taking off in a fifty-horsepower Curtiss plane from a wooden platform constructed on the cruiser *Birmingham,* anchored at Hampton Roads, Virginia. On January 18, 1911, Ely lands and takes off from the armored cruiser *Pennsylvania,* at anchor in San Francisco Bay.

On February 17, 1911, Curtiss lands a hydroplane alongside the *Pennsylvania.* Curtiss' craft is hoisted aboard and off again by ship's crane, proving hydroplanes can operate with ships of the fleet.

Little do Ellyson, Ely, and Curtiss know their first demonstration launches a long adventure that grows into giant aircraft carriers, supersonic jets, the crucible of combat and shots to the moon.

But their pioneering adventures convince Congress, which appropriates $25,000 for experimental work in naval aeronautics. The Navy purchases one Wright and two Curtiss flying machines on May 8, 1911, a date the Navy recognizes as the beginning of naval aviation. In September 1911, Lieutenants Ellyson (No. 1), John Rodgers (No. 2), and John M. Towers (No. 3) finish flying instruction. And on October 7, 1911, thirteen days before Pensacola's scheduled decommissioning, Secretary of the Navy Josephus Daniels appoints a board of officers to develop "a comprehensive plan for the organization of a Naval Aeronautic Service."

Worried Pensacola businessmen are unaware of the aeroplane; still wracked by the devastating 1906 hurricane that shatters the port and crippled by the rapidly declining timber trade, they frightfully search for new avenues to offset the feared economic loss of the Navy Yard. They turn to agriculture; they lack facilities for promoting tourism and industry; they still dream of rebuilding port wharves and promoting new marine commerce. They cling to hope for reviving shipbuilding with surplus facilities at the dormant Navy Yard.

In 1912, with opening of the Panama Canal, Pensacolians again are encouraged by the harbor's potential for Gulf and foreign commerce. Pensacola is one hundred miles nearer Panama than Mobile; two hundred miles nearer than Galveston; three hundred miles nearer than New Orleans. But again Pensacola drifts in its nature-endowed Florida isolation.

Touring the yard in 1913, Secretary Daniels lifts Pensacolians' expectations. He says the Navy should reopen the base in anticipation of the impact of the canal. Still, they are unsure when Assistant Secretary of the Navy Franklin Delano Roosevelt visits the dormant yard. They anticipate possibly a detachment of Marines.

But on January 2, 1914, a surprising Associated Press news report from Washington headlines *The Daily News* and *Pensacola Journal:* "Air craft soon will form a great part of the naval force of the United States, Secretary Daniels so announced in outlining plans for systematic experiments on a large scale with aeroplanes." Daniels "approved the naval board's recommendation that Pensacola, Fla., be made an aeronautical center. A permanent flying school will be located there with Lieutenant Commander Henry C. Mustin in charge. Trials will be located from the deck of the battleship *Mississippi* in that harbor. Captain Mark L. Bristol is assigned to have charge of the study and development of this branch of the service and the matter of purchasing many dirigibles will be taken up and many aeroplanes bought by the Navy department."

Already a small legion of Navy fliers had demonstrated the operational capabilities of aircraft and stimulated interest in aviation during fleet maneuvers at Guantanamo Bay, Cuba, in January 1913.

On January 10, 1914, the Navy's aviation unit from Annapolis—nine officers, twenty-three enlisted men, seven kitelike seaplanes, and portable hangars—arrive aboard the battleship USS *Mississippi* and the collier *Orion* to establish a flying school. Lieutenant Towers commands the flying unit; Commander Mustin, station commandant, on the cutting edge of change, is ordered to plan for the Navy's future in the skies.

The birdmen waste no time.

Undaunted by Pensacola harbor obstacles, Lieutenant Towers and Ensign Godfrey de C. Chevalier wing over Bayou Grande and Pensacola Bay at an altitude of eight hundred to one thousand feet for twenty minutes in the first flight in the State of Florida on February 2, 1914—thirteen days after arrival. Chevalier then goes aloft for a fifteen-minute flight with his student, Lieutenant Commander Roper, who was airborne the first time. Towers and Mustin then team for the third experiment, their cockpit instrument reading eight hundred feet.

A *Pensacola Journal* reporter shares the spectators' excitement:

All of the rises and landings, which were made from and on the water respectively, were perfectly executed. The atmospheric conditions were ideal for aeronautics. At one time the aviators came over a point near the western portion of the city and disappeared to the northward. The machines in the air look like gigantic buzzards and make a noise plainly audible on the ground as the airmen pass over. The speed attained is remarkable being much greater than that of a buzzard or hawk in flight. In descending the aviators experience until they become used to flying, a feeling of nausea like unto that feeling one has when descending rapidly in an elevator.

But on February 6, 1914, Pensacolians watch their first aerial crash in horror as Lieutenant J. M. Murray plunges in his hydro-aeroplane into Pensacola Bay from an altitude of two hundred feet and drowns amid the wreckage. The unlucky thirty-year-old pilot holding certificate No. 13 is the Navy's second aeronautical fatality.

Five submarines arrive to conduct experimental operations with aircraft, but on April 20, 1914, the Pensacola airmen are ordered to implement President Woodrow Wilson's orders for American naval forces to seize the customs house in Vera Cruz. Pensacola's intrepid beginners aloft in their contraptions over Vera Cruz and Tampico in Mexico provide the first air support for a foreign patrol action.

Just as the Mexican War had created feverish activity at the Navy Yard in 1845, the fliers are drawn into a simmering dispute with Mexico fol-

lowing the arrest of Americans from the USS *Dolphin* seeking supplies ashore at Tampico. The Wilson administration and Congress support unilateral action by the American naval commander, who demands a formal apology, punishment for the responsible officer, and a twenty-one-gun salute for the American flag. Two aviation detachments, each composed of two or three young and cheerful pilots, aviation mechanics and two hydroplanes, make American history, responding effectively during the forty-three day scouting expedition. On May 6, 1914, rifle fire strikes one of the American craft on reconnaissance near Vera Cruz—the first mark of combat on a U.S. Navy plane, although American pilots didn't fire a shot, suffer any injuries or noticeably affect the Vera Cruz incident. They return to Pensacola in mid-June.

On July 1, 1914, naval aviation is formally recognized by the Office of Naval Aeronautics; in November the old Navy Yard is officially designated the Pensacola Naval Aeronautical Station, the nation's first and only installation for flight training and experimental flying until the outbreak of World War I in April 1917.

The station has other pre-war *firsts:* Lt. Patrick Bellinger, piloting the AB-2 flying boat, is successfully catapulted from a Navy coal barge in Pensacola Bay on April 16, 1915; Commandant Mustin makes the first catapult launching from a ship, flying off the stern of the armored cruiser *North Carolina* anchored in Pensacola Bay in November 1915; Richard C. Saufley climbs to an altitude record of 16,072 feet in a hydroplane in March 1916.

But fatalities and storms mar the early training. In June 1916, Lieutenant Saufley, Naval Aviator No. 14, dies in a crash during an endurance test over Santa Rosa Island after being aloft eight hours and fifty-one minutes. On July 5, 1916, another Gulf hurricane wrecks planes, wharves, overhead wires, roads, the railroad across Bayou Grande, and damages buildings. Quickly rebuilding, the station by the end of 1916 employs 400 civilians serving a naval complement of fifty-eight officers, 431 enlisted men, thirty-three seaplanes, one kite balloon, one free balloon, and one non-rigid balloon.

Yet Washington attitudes about flying remain skeptical, even if the young Pensacola fliers are showing the nation air power is here to stay.

With naval aviation a new-fangled military tool, early aviators steering primitive craft learn their lessons by making their own rules. Aero-

Old Navy Yard.
John C. Pace Library, University
of West Florida

Commandant's Quarters built in
1874 still remain at today's Naval
Air Station.
Pensacola Historical Society

A seaplane being readied for a catapult launch. Planes such as this one
were launched from cruisers and
landed on the water. They were then
hoisted back aboard by crane.
U.S. Navy photo

First class of aviators, Pensacola stand-
ing left to right are Paunack, Spencer,
Bartlett, Edwards, Bronson, Corry,
Norfleet, McDonald, and Scofield. Sit-
ting are Saufley, Bellinger, Whiting,
Mustin, Read, Johnson, Cunningham,
Evans, and Haas.
U.S. Navy photo

nauts grow their wings by trial and error; they experience exhilaration, danger, strangeness, and fear perched on the edge of a wing, dangling their feet down to a bar on a pontoon or hunching and praying over wobbly little seaplanes up off the water, feeling as if "sitting on top of the world."

In the beginning, appropriations are meager, training loosely organized. Not until 1915 do the experimenting airmen have a definitive syllabus for flight training. Aviators need only ten hours for gold wings, and the training program runs from dawn to dusk seven days a week.

But it's still seat-of-the-pants flying; student aviators only spend twenty-five to fifty hours airborne and only have to appear able to "go it alone" to receive wings. Students learn the importance of maintaining an air speed causing the aircraft's wires to whistle sharply. They develop their own gauge: "If the wires don't sing, the angels will!"

Congress remains reluctant to expand the flying service beyond Pensacola's feeble beginning until it declares war on Germany in 1917. But, soon one hundred new structures—ranging from seaplane hangars to barracks—change the face of the station during the war years. The Navy trains 921 naval aviators, sixty-three dirigible pilots, fifteen free balloon pilots, and 5,382 aviation mechanics before the Armistice November 11, 1918. Commanded by Lt. Kenneth Whiting, Naval Aviator No. 16, the Pensacola-trained First Aeronautic Detachment is the first United States military unit sent to Europe, arriving June 1917. Renamed the Pensacola Naval Air Station on December 17, 1917, the old Navy Yard with 438 officers and 5,559 enlisted men is firmly established as the nation's first and largest of the seven established across the nation; indeed, considered largest in the world when peace returns. Boosted by an efficient Naval Air Reserve program, the new air station expands beyond boundaries of the old Navy Yard, diminishing the villages of Woolsey and Warrington.

As the *giant buzzards* multiply, the old village of Woolsey is razed for Station Field runways to handle land planes then replacing hydroplanes. Formerly used for blimp operations, Station Field is destined to be enlarged and named Chevalier Field in honor of one of the first two pilots to fly at Pensacola—Godfrey de C. Chevalier, Aviator No. 7.

In 1922, the city of Pensacola and Chamber of Commerce provide the Navy Department with a landing field five miles north of the city. Dedicated on December 17, 1922, the facility located in the vicinity of East Texar Drive is named Corry Field, after Medal of Honor winner William M. Corry, Jr., Naval Aviator No. 23, first Floridian to enter flight training at Pensacola.

In 1922, the collier USS *Jupiter* is converted into the Navy's first aircraft carrier and renamed the USS *Langley* (CV-1), for one of aviation's founders. Experimental operations by the *Langley* in Pensacola waters during 1923 and 1924 influence the conversion of unfinished cruisers *Saratoga* and *Lexington* to aircraft carriers.

Enlarging classes and formalizing training programs, Pensacola NAS begins its first class of enlisted pilots, who earn gold wings. The young Pensacola pilots are inspired by two visits by barnstorming pilot Charles Lindbergh, who stops for repairs in early 1920 and returns in October 1927 to express his appreciation during a cross-country tour following his historic trans-Atlantic flight. He arrives in the aftermath of the 1926 hurricane, which had covered the station with five feet of water, requiring three years for repairs.

Yet the Navy in the 1920s needs to expand Station Field and Corry Field. Boxed in at Corry Field, with inadequate facilities at both landing fields, the Navy considers abandoning Pensacola. Alerted by Charles P. Mason of the Bureau of Aeronautics, Pensacola businessmen and the Escambia County Commissioners join in the purchase of five hundred acres west of the city for the new Corry Field, dedicated in July 1927.

The Navy Department requests $5 million from Congress for modernization of the station, but the onslaught of the Great Depression throws military spending into a tailspin. And naval aviation does not escape cutbacks. Shortage of funds curtails training; no new students are ordered at Pensacola NAS from August 1932 to June 1933.

In 1930-31 old Warrington at the gates of the station is relocated north of Bayou Grande for expanding flight training requirements.

Even though Japan rejects naval disarmament in 1936, and begins building a war machine, Washington does not change policy. President Franklin D. Roosevelt had promised to cut the budget deficit during the 1936 election campaign; after the election, all Navy Department bureaus are ordered to trim their budgets. But Pensacola's training program gets a healthy boost when Congress authorizes the designation

The USS Jupiter was converted into the first aircraft carrier and renamed the USS Langley.
U.S. Navy photo

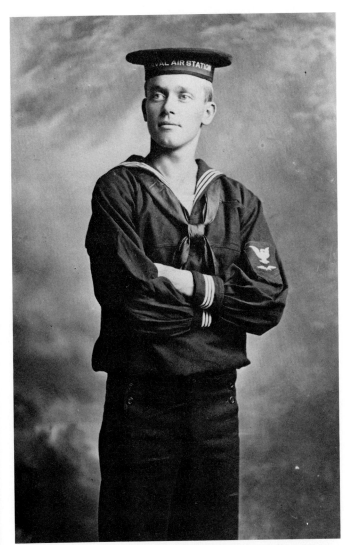

Unidentified sailor whose portrait was taken by local photographer H. Lee Bell sometime after 1916.
Pensacola Historical Society

Unidentified black aviator whose photo was also taken by H. Lee Bell.
Pensacola Historical Society

of student fliers as Naval Aviation Cadets, and a congressional bill providing for three thousand useful naval aircraft is signed into law on May 18, 1938. New facilities at Pensacola, financed by millions of dollars expended in emergency relief projects of the Works Progress Administration and the Public Works Administration, mark the preparation of Pensacola NAS for the vigorous training program on the horizon.

Public works projects construct schools for aviation mechanics, flight instruction, aerial photography and aviation medicine. Station Field, expanded to 180 acres, is formally dedicated and renamed Chevalier Field on December 30, 1936. The Navy builds a dispensary and new hospital, Marine barracks, and extensive assembly and repair shops—improvements enhancing naval aviation's preparedness for World War II.

Governmental expenditures provide jobs and fatten Pensacola's economy—especially after President Roosevelt visits the city and naval facilities in 1938. Greeted by large crowds along Pensacola streets, Roosevelt charms the city, saying, "I am keen about this place, I am keen about its people, and I am keen about its future." As a result of Roosevelt's visit, the Pensacola Housing Authority receives federal funds for the first two public projects, Aragon and Attucks Courts, and off-base military housing at Moreno Court. In 1938, student pilots train at the Pensacola Naval Air Station, Corry Field, and fifteen auxiliary and emergency landing fields dotting the West Florida and South Alabama countryside.

Roosevelt visits Pensacola four times—in 1914 to help launch naval aviation; three times as president. In February 1940—under tight security—the President rides in a downtown parade along Gregory, Palafox and Garden streets and Barrancas Avenue and boards the cruiser *Tuscaloosa* at Pensacola NAS for a ten-day fishing vacation in the Gulf. The *Pensacola Journal,* headlining Roosevelt's visit, speculates the sighting of foreign submarines in the Gulf prompted the increased security for the man who would be the last commander-and-chief to visit Pensacola.

After the Japanese attack on Pearl Harbor, the Navy accelerates training at Chevalier Field and Corry and Saufley auxiliary flying fields, and constructs Ellyson Field, commemorating Theodore G. Ellyson, the first naval aviator. By 1943, student pilots train at Bronson Field, named for Clarence King Bronson; Barin Field

(Louis T. Barin); and Whiting Field near Milton, named by Kenneth Whiting.

Realigning the training command in 1942, the Navy establishes the Naval Air Training Center and creates central administration for the Pensacola station, six auxiliary bases and Navy Hospital, and the schools of aviation medicine and photography. Even though other stations, such as Jacksonville and Corpus Christi expand the Navy's flight training, Pensacola remains the center for aviation medicine and photographic training. Thousands of pilots train in Pensacola; in 1944, the peak war training year, 12,000 pilots earn wings, flying a combined total of almost two million hours; in May alone, the training fields produce 1,411 pilots.

For the first time in military history, naval engagements are fought entirely in the air. Aircraft carriers—signalled by the first designed and built carrier, USS *Ranger* (CV-4), in 1934—are vital elements in fleet warfare strategy. Within nine days after Pearl Harbor, the Pensacola training program increases from eight hundred a year to a yearly enrollment of twenty-five hundred. From the beginning, Pensacola's wartime training has a British—and later—international flavor. The first class of one hundred British fliers and thirty aerial observers arrive in July 1941. Later Free French and other Allied countries send student pilots through the training program. Enduring friendships develop as Pensacolians invite the British flight students for Sunday dinners, family activities, and holiday outings. The last class—seventeen aviators—depart Pensacola in December 1944. But the *limeys* retain Pensacola ties with annual reunions of the British Pensacola Veterans Association in London, organize nostalgic pilgrimages to Pensacola, and plan a Golden Anniversary Reunion in Pensacola in 1999.

Women begin a new era for Pensacola Navy when the first WAVE officer, Mary B. Pine, begins duty as dispensary chemist in November 1942, and enlisted WAVES Ruth Gump and Lois Barringer arrive for hospital service within four months. In December 1943, there are one thousand women in uniform at Pensacola NAS. The wartime WAVES, of course, pioneer the eventual integration of women into all facets of Navy service—including naval aviation—during the last quarter of the twentieth century.

By V-J day ending World War II, Pensacola NAS has its sealegs, maturing in its reputation as the Cradle of Naval Aviation. Pensacola bases

View of the Naval Air Station May 4, 1918, showing recent storm damage done to the south shore.
U.S. Navy photo

Another view taken May 4, 1918, gives a good view of the World War I camouflaged buildings.
U.S. Navy photo

Workers from the machinery division at NAS posed for the photographer in 1918.
Pensacola Historical Society

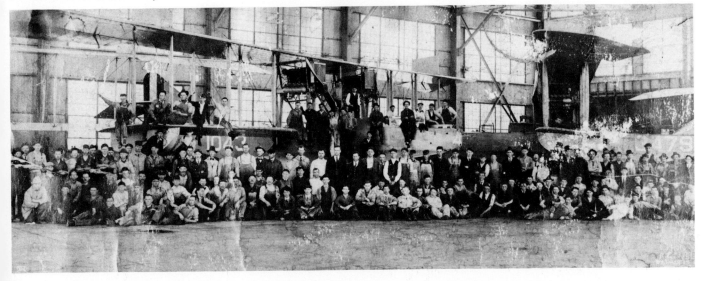

train 28,562 pilots during the 1941-1945 war years. Navy and Marine aircraft destroy more than fifteen thousand enemy aircraft, sink 161 Japanese warships, and destroy sixty-three German submarines.

Rapid development of air warfare in World War II signals the end of Army coastal defenses; the Coastal Artillery is abolished as a separate Army service, and the Post of Fort Barrancas is declared obsolete in 1947. The Navy gains control of the Army Reservation. In 1971, the harbor fortifications become historical landmarks administered by the National Park Service as elements of Gulf Islands National Seashore. Other Barrancas facilities, including the National Cemetery, become part of the Naval Air Station.

In the post-war 1940s, Naval Aviation is respected as a vital arm of naval warfare, symbolized by the creation of Navy's own precision team of flying diplomats, organized at Jacksonville on April 18, 1946, and eventually named Blue Angels for the famous bistro. They appear for the first time in Pensacola on July 10, 1946, but their second home base is Corpus Christi, Texas. Generations of the ever-sharp Blue Angels, the Navy's flight demonstration team based at Pensacola NAS after June 1955, go from propellor-driven aircraft to supersonic jet, carrying the message of Naval Aviation with precision performances in the skies across America.

In 1948, the Naval Air Basic Training Command Headquarters moves from Corpus Christi to Pensacola, setting in motion an expansion that includes new aircraft designed strictly for training, from propeller to jet. During the Korean Conflict, the Navy adjusted to the transition from propellers to jet, turning out six thousand aviators from 1950 to 1953. In early 1955, Pensacola NAS opens its jetport, Forrest Sherman Field, where during the 1960s and 1970s pilots train for the hearty demands of the Vietnam War.

Helicopters prove their value in the Korean Conflict and Vietnam, and busy Whiting Field near Milton emerges as headquarters for one of the Navy's largest training wings for basic and advance flight training and helicopter instruction. Training activity at Whiting in the 1980s is compared with the traffic at major civilian airports at Chicago, Atlanta, and Los Angeles.

In 1962, the USS Antietam—eighth carrier assigned to training in Pensacola waters—sails away as the fabled "Blue Ghost" of World War II, the USS Lexington, homeports in Pensacola as the Navy's only training carrier. Fresh

from her last fleet sea duty action in the Cuban missile crisis, the "Lady Lex" becomes a popular Navy symbol, her ocean voyages behind, engines retooled, guns silent; her steel chest lined with war-campaign ribbons from two-and-one-half years of combat that brought her eleven battle stars and a Presidential Unit Citation.

Less than twenty years earlier, the Lexington had destroyed more than 850 enemy planes and sank or damaged 900,000 tons of enemy shipping in the Pacific during World War II. First commissioned in 1943, and recommissioned in 1955 with an angled deck and modern aviation equipment, the Lexington alternates between Far East deployments and West Coast carrier qualification operations for fleet pilots before becoming the Pensacola training carrier and amassing an array of naval aviation records, including more than 445,000 arrested landings in 1963.

Besides the Antietam, Pensacola pilots train on the Monterey, Cabot, Wright, Saipan, Ranger, Guadalcanal, and the experimental Langley.

The Lexington arrives the year the secretary of the Navy authorizes the United States Naval Aviation Museum to reflect the development, growth, and historic heritage of United States naval aviation. With community, state, and corporate financial support, museum founders move from an 8,500 square-foot World War II building to a newly constructed museum facility, dedicated on April 13, 1975. The civilian booster organization, Naval Aviation Museum Association, becomes a national foundation in 1975, envisioning a constantly expanding shrine that salutes air pioneers and heroes, and expands the collections of ancient hydroplanes, canvas-shawled jennies, World War II gunships, Jet Age aircraft, and spacecraft scarred by war and orbital discovery.

In 1965, Chevalier Field is closed as a landing strip and becomes the heliport for West Florida's largest industry, the Naval Air Rework Facility. Known as NARF, the center in the 1980s employs thirty-six hundred civilian technicians in aircraft repair.

Congressman Robert L. F. (Bob) Sikes, a Crestview weekly newspaperman who follows retiring Milton lawyer Millard Caldwell to Congress in 1940, becomes the influential Washington champion of the massive buildup of Navy and Air Force training along the West Florida coast from Pensacola to Panama City during his thirty-eight years representing Florida's First Congressional District.

Calling himself West Florida's "He-Coon,"

President Franklin D. Roosevelt and
Captain Aubrey W. Fitch, comman-
dant of the Naval Air Station, inspect
the base, August 1938.
John C. Pace Library, University of
West Florida

World War II war bond advertisement.
Pensacola Historical Society

Pontoon training plane at NAS in the
1930s.
T. T. Wentworth, Jr.

Sikes rises in seniority on the House Armed Services Committee and becomes chairman of the House Subcommittee on Military Appropriations. Aligning with other Southern Democrats championing national defense, Sikes protects and expands the Pensacola naval complex from the wartime forties until his retirement in 1978. He fends off congressional critics who try to ground the Blue Angels and unify Navy and Army helicopter training at Fort Rucker, Alabama. He defends West Florida bases in the fierce political competition between Pensacola and Texas installations. Sikes' successor, Earl Hutto, of Panama City, follows the He-Coon's protective tradition as Navy and Air Force defender. Yet in the 1980s new training concepts begun during Sikes' last congressional years of the 1970s continue realigning Florida and Texas flight training missions.

In 1971, the Pentagon creates the headquarters for the Chief of Naval Education and Training at Pensacola NAS and relocates the Chief of Naval Aviation Training headquarters at Corpus Christi. The sweeping new Pensacola command—pioneered by its first commander, Vice Adm. Malcom W. (Chris) Cagle—combines the direction and control of all Navy schools and training programs worldwide, including naval aviation.

In 1985, the Navy pins the last wings of aviators graduating from Pensacola NAS; the reorganized training program places advanced flight training duties at Texas and Mississippi bases. Yet Pensacola NAS on the eve of the 1990s remains a myriad of naval aviation activity. Besides training air wings and subordinate squadrons and headquartering the Naval Aviation Schools Command, the Pensacola station represents a multi-billion-dollar economy in the Pensacola area with the Pensacola Naval Aerospace Medical Institute and Research Laboratory and eight-story 310-bed Naval Hospital, aircraft repair at NARF, Corry Station Naval Technical Training Center for cryptology, electronic warfare, and photography instruction, and the Saufley Field Naval Education and Training Development Center.

In 1985, a new concept—homeporting twenty-nine ships of the Navy fleet in nine Gulf Coast ports—rallies Pensacolians to work for the big prize, the battleship USS *Wisconsin* surface action group. But the Navy chooses Corpus Christi for the battleship group and assigns the operational carrier USS *Kitty Hawk* and a mine

warfare ship to Pensacola for the 1990s. In the realignment, the Navy's only training carrier, Pensacola-based USS *Lexington* will homeport at the new Corpus Christi naval base.

Yet the Pensacola Naval Supply Center, established in 1985, serves as a vital homeporting pipeline as the ship-supply distribution center for naval facilities along the Gulf Coast and throughout the Southeast.

The old Navy Yard that grew into Pensacola Naval Air Station enters the 1990s with a long and adventurous heritage, with major contributions to the ever-developing science of naval aviation, and defense of the nation. Since the beginning of Pensacola's air age in 1914, the Navy remains an integral part of the community that generations of aviators speak of reverently as the "Mother-in-law to the U.S. Navy."

Elsewhere, across the city, the influence of the Navy flavors Pensacola: from the decayed and abandoned Hotel San Carlos—once a social gathering place for Navy pilots, flight students, sailors and Marines who court and marry Pensacola girls—to the B and B Cafe, Child's Restaurant, and Saenger Theatre on busy Palafox Street. From the World War I hangars and concrete launching ramps for seaplanes once forming a flight flotilla in Pensacola Bay to Mustin Beach Officers' Club, where World War II fliers danced with Pensacola girls to the Big Band music of the 1940s. World War II and Korean Conflict veterans fondly remember the popular restaurants: Bartel's, known for fried chicken and home-made wine; Martine's on Mobile Highway at the Circle; and Carpenter's on Barrancas Avenue in Warrington.

They remember the steady parade of entertainers and celebrities at the Naval Air Station and visiting the community: film actress Mary Pickford visiting her uniformed husband, film actor Charles (Buddy) Rogers (star of Hollywood's pioneering aviation film, *Wings*), Florida-born comedienne/singer Judy Canova, golfer Patty Berg, Helen Keller, actor Tyrone Power, boxing legend Jack Dempsey, sailor/actor Leif Erickson (who marries a Pensacolian and makes his second home here during a long post-war movie and television career, including the role of Big John Cannon in the TV series, "High Chapperal"), actress Laraine Day, Hollywood comedy actor Andy Devine, radio personality Arthur Godfrey (who discovered singer Julius La Rosa at the naval station), and the Bob Hope troupe—with Jerry Colonna, Francis Langford,

Yeomanettes who volunteered for Navy service during World War I. They worked largely in clerical positions and were disbanded after the war. In World War II women again volunteered for Navy service and became known as WAVES.
Pensacola Historical Society

The USS Lexington AUT 16, homeported in Pensacola for many years, serves as the Navy's training carrier.
U.S. Navy photo

A formation of SNJs flies over Pensacola. One of the many "sea stories" about this plane dealt with the custom of "booming the tower." When jet aircraft first broke the sound barrier the resulting sonic boom startled many unwary citizens. Eglin Air Force Base received the first jet aircraft in the West Florida region. Pilots enjoyed breaking the sound barrier while flying past the control tower at Eglin. To avoid surprising the tower crew (and hurting their ear drums) pilots were advised to request permission to "boom the tower" prior to the actual event. Naval aviators at Pensacola, flying propeller driven SNJs, were naturally aware, as well as envious, of this procedure. On one occasion the Eglin tower crew heard the familiar radio request, "Permission to boom the tower." Asked to identify his aircraft, the pilot replied, "Secret Navy jet requests permission to boom the tower." The curious airman replied, "Permission granted." The plane normally flew by the tower within seconds of the permission granted message. In this case many minutes went by and nothing happened. The airman questioned the pilot, "Secret Navy jet, are you prepared to boom the tower?" The answer came back, "Secret Navy jet approaching the tower. Will boom in approximately five minutes." This represented a lengthening of the usual time but the airman did not withdraw permission. In five minutes the SNJ came into view of the tower. As he drew even with the tower, the navy pilot radioed in a loud voice, "Boom."
U.S. Navy Photo

and Skinny Ennis and his orchestra—broadcasting their popular radio show from Pensacola in 1943.

And in the early 1950s, Martin (Trader Jon) Weissman, former saloonkeeper in the Florida Keys, wins Navy affection and becomes a part of the naval aviation legend with a popular bay-front bistro in a 1886 ship chandlery building at 511 South Palafox Street. Pilots in Navy blue and Marine green share late-night flying stories as wine flows in the cluttered old saloon amid tons of memorabilia tracing heroes and romance of naval aviation.

Marine and Navy astronauts John Glenn and Alan Shepard; British Prince Andrew; and actors John Wayne, Dan Dailey, Charlton Heston, and Ernest Borgnine are among the many celebrated visitors who bend elbows at Trader Jon's bar. Along with the Blue Angels, who honor Weissman, Bob Hope, and Borgnine as Honorary Blue Angels, the Navy's top brass—admirals, Navy secretaries, and celebrated jet jockeys—share flying stories at Trader's bar. Bob Hope put Trader Jon's on national television by staging a comic scene depicting the South Palafox bar in his "75th Naval Aviation Anniversary" show in 1986.

Hollywood filmmakers discover Pensacola is an ideal location for shooting flying scenes for some of the popular aviation movies in the 1930s and 1940s. The film era signals the end of pacifism, air progress, and the big-buildup for America's entry in the World War II.

Warner Brothers cameramen first capture aerial footage in Pensacola for *Dawn Patrol,* the 1938 classic with the all-British cast headed by Errol Flynn, David Niven, and Basil Rathbone battling the feared German aces in World War I.

And in July 1938, fifty-three Warner Brothers actors, directors, and technicians arrive in Pensacola to film *Wings of the Navy,* starring leading men George Brent and John Payne, leading lady Olivia de Haviland, and comedian Frank McHugh. The Hollywood entourage, occupying thirty-five suites in Hotel San Carlos, enlivens the city with promotional appearances before settling into the closed-set filming at the air station during the twelve-day visit. Autograph seekers, teenagers, and film buffs haunt the San Carlos lobby, ogling the film stars; actors and crew relax at Pensacola Beach and go deep-sea fishing. Mayor L. C. Hagler proclaims "Wings of the Navy Week," launching a city-wide sales promotion; teenager Shirley Sexton wears the crown

of "Miss Wings of the Navy," and the *Journal* applauds the national spotlight being focused on the city through radio broadcasts featuring the film's stars. A *Journal* society page columnist observes the furor over the celebrated movie-makers "even eclipsed the visit to the area by President Roosevelt."

On February 3, 1938, townspeople and Navy officials pack the Saenger Theatre for Pensacola's first world movie premiere of what Capt. Aubrey Fitch, station commandant, describes as a "touching tribute to the Navy." At a time when President Roosevelt was trying to persuade Congress to increase Navy allocations, Fitch says the film—coupled with FDR's Pensacola visit—will "play a stirring role in support for the Navy." Although none of the cast was present for the premiere, there were many telegrams from Hollywood, including director Lloyd Bacon's tribute: "If any city deserves gold flying wings, that city is Pensacola."

In the 1941 Warner Brothers film, *Dive Bomber,* swashbuckler Errol Flynn, Fred MacMurray, and Ralph Bellamy are in skies over Pensacola, San Diego, and the carrier USS *Enterprise* with their earth-bound eyes on leading lady Alexis Smith. And for the 1957 John Wayne-Maureen O'Hara film, *Wings of Eagles,* director John Ford uses the old Navy flying boat area, Mustin Beach Officers Club, a Bayshore residence, and a Pensacola Regional Airport hangar for scenes depicting the early daredevil flying career of Navy Comdr. Frank (Spig) Wead. Wayne portrays Wead, who became a Hollywood screenwriter after a crippling injury ended his Navy flying career. Wead helps sell Hollywood and the nation on naval aviation and serves as a special Navy adviser for World War II carrier warfare.

The training carrier USS *Lexington* wins film star rank in 1970s and 1980s, twice helping re-create the World War II Battle of Midway Island in the Gulf of Mexico. For the American Revolution Bicentennial, Hollywood's *Midway* (1976) is partially filmed aboard the Lady Lex with stars Charleston Heston, Henry Fonda, Glenn Ford, and Robert Mitchum. And in 1987, television producers transform the carrier into vintage 1940s gray and hide its slanted 884-foot training deck for jets from camera lens to film battle scenes for the thirty-hour TV miniseries "War and Remembrance" based on the Herman Wouk novel. Once again, for the TV sequel "The Winds of War," the Lady Lex sails the Gulf with

Sailors strolling a downtown Pensacola street.
Pensacola Historical Society

Pensacola has been called the "Mother-in-law of the Navy." This young couple might explain why.
Pensacola Historical Society

The famed "Blue Angels" over the USS Lexington at Pensacola NAS.
Pensacola Historical Society

Navy Hellcats and dive bombers aboard, and Japanese Zeros and dive bombers in the sky. And her dummy guns belch propane flames in a Hollywood mock battle reminiscent of the real combat experience of the *Blue Ghost*—the ship that could not be sunk.

Indeed, the Lady Lex, doing daily duty as a floating runway for carrier-landing training or refitted and repainted as a World War II ghost for Hollywood filmmakers, conveys a theater of airmen and seamen at war during her long Pensacola adventure.

Tugs—tiny in the great shadow of the Lady Lex—cruise alongside the big floating city of 1,500 officers and men and women, pulling the carrier into the Pensacola harbor channel for another routine training mission. Once in the Gulf, operating fifty miles at sea, airmen hasten into readiness for flight operations.

Helicopters hang whirling above as flight crews police the deck for debris that might be sucked into the jet turbines. They scurry like football players in bright orange colors and noise-muffling helmets breaking from huddles into broken-field running. They prepare two-men fire trucks, adjust landing devices and await the first bird to drop from the sky after its run from Forrest Sherman Field.

And then, yonder in the blue, it begins: a symphony of winged flight, jetbirds circling and finding the landing pattern; they thunder onto the old, scarred wooden deck. One by one the birds are caught snugly in a steel catcher's mitt. And just as quickly, as an army of flight attendants busy as Indianapolis pit-stop mechanics nurse deck operations, they're off again.

A deck-top slingshot propels the jetbirds skyward—in three seconds, off the 221-foot track; suddenly they are gone only to come again and again in the perpetual din of shrill jet noise amid the pungency of jetfuel exhaust that forces itself, hurricane-like, through the hanging, humid vapors of the sea air.

There is the curling cadence of the bluewater Gulf beneath the steady knifing presence of a runway at sea; and in the sky young student pilots search for the postage-stamp landing strip they must find and master if they are to win their Navy Wings of Gold.

It's Pensacola's *own* adventure—the U.S. Navy; and, from 1914 until the decade of the 1990s the evolution of Navy flight weaves a strong legacy for new generations testing man-made wings above the sands of history in Pensacola harbor.

Bob Hope and Elizabeth Taylor performed aboard the USS Lexington *during the celebration of the seventy-fifth anniversary of naval aviation in 1986.*
Pensacola News-Journal *Files*

*Inside the U.S. Naval Aviation
Museum.
U.S. Navy photo*

*Bob Hope and Don Johnson at naval
aviation celebration.*
Pensacola News-Journal *Files*

Aerial of Pensacola waterfront circa 1927.
Pensacola Historical Society

PART

10

The New Pensacola

Touted as America's Naples, America's Riviera, and Queen City of the Gulf, the first New Pensacola rises from Colonel Chipley's old seaport in the city-building new-century years before World War I.

With the harbor dredged to a depth of thirty-three feet, and a port only six miles from the entrance to the harbor, Pensacola investors awaken to voices of a New South in the first decade. Charles Bliss's *Quarterly* declares the harbor big enough to accommodate all the navies of the world. The flagship *Kearsage,* battleships *Maine, Massachusetts,* and *Alabama,* and the North Atlantic Squadron rendezvous in the bay. Warships stage gunnery practice and maneuvers in the Gulf.

Heeding Frank L. Mayes' *Journal* boosterism, they realistically tie their city's economic future to the U.S. Navy, and the port's ability to attract local manufacture. Yet troubling changes are in the wind: diminishing timber resources, wreckage from Gulf storms, the emergence of Mobile and New Orleans, and reliance on only one rail carrier, the company that had built the port— L & N Railroad.

In 1900, the Deep Water City of 17,747 people moves on gas-lighted sandbed streets except for the noisy brick-paved surface of Palafox Street from Main to Garden. Water is pumped by a private company from deep wells at Palafox

and Cervantes streets; two large sandy ditches along Palafox carry run-off directly to the bay. North Hill and East Hill are growing, but most Pensacolians live south of Gregory Street.

Yet, from 1906 to 1912, a building boom stirs expectations. With population totaling nearly twenty-three thousand, creosoted wooden paving blocks over twenty-one miles of city streets, and concrete sidewalks replace condemned wooden pathways. New downtown construction lifts spirits and the skyline: three-story fireproof $200,000 F. C. Brent Building, seven-story $200,000 W. A. Blount building, ten-story American National Bank "skyscraper," Spanish Renaissance $100,000 City Hall on Jefferson Street facing Plaza Ferdinand, and the half-million-dollar, eight-story Hotel San Carlos. In the shadow of the skyscraper, graceful white marble and granite facings and fluted columns of First National Bank's Greek temple architecture reflect splendor of the downtown transformation.

The Spanish-style San Carlos with imposing iron balconies, stands elegantly amidst wide parkways on the Palafox-Garden corner in 1910, erasing embarrassment for poor hotel accommodations for travelers and prospective investors. Partially built by Pensacolians subscribing $152,000 and $200,000 from a bond issue, it's Florida's largest, and touted by manager George Hervey as the South's finest. From upper floors, guests see Santa Rosa Island beyond storm-damaged bay wharves, and new classical or Greek Revival homes joining the Queen Anne residences of North Hill.

Between 1906 and 1909, new downtown construction totals $3 million; by 1912, another half-million dollars go into construction of the yellow-brick L & N Depot, replacing the 1882 Union Station; Cudahy and Armour and Company Building, Bon Marche Store, Keyser building, and other business edifices. Landmark buildings spreading from Plaza Ferdinand to streets crossing upper Palafox establish the basic character of Pensacola downtown business until after World War I. By the end of the Progressive Era (1900-1918), Pensacola has a lighted "White Way" business district from Main to Wright on Palafox and from Baylen and Jefferson to Garden. Public-spirited volunteers inspire recreational programs, especially Bayview Park on Bayou Texar, and help the city commission employ St. Louis city planner and landscapist George E. Kessler to beautify streets, develop parks, and create parkways on Garden, upper Palafox, and Wright streets. Trolley tracks are removed from the center of Palafox, and Kessler encourages planting of palm trees along the main thoroughfare. The *Journal* predicts "Pensacola will no doubt be the prettiest city in the South."

The Chamber of Commerce, real estate promoters, Frank L. Mayes' *Journal,* Charles Bliss's *Quarterly,* and Hotel San Carlos manager George Hervey emphasize the "New Pensacola."

Gulf Beach Highway (1916-1923) carries visitors to Gulf beaches on Foster's Island (Perdido Key), and prompts the beginning of the three-hundred-room Gulf Beach Hotel in 1925. But—abandoned after the devastating 1926 hurricane and collapse of the Florida land boom—the hotel's bleaching concrete bones survive as a skeleton of failed dreams.

Northward, the concrete Star Route 7 (1926) links with Alabama at Flomaton, and opening of the Escambia River bridge (1926) heightens hopes for building "Old Spanish Trail" across West Florida, linking Marianna with Mobile, through Pensacola. In 1931, Lillian Bridge spans Perdido Bay, connecting Pensacola with Alabama, spurring hopes for connecting the port with Baldwin County agricultural markets. Pensacola's unique Scenic Highway, stretching across the red-clay bluffs along Escambia Bay, links the city on the east with the new Escambia River Bridge. And on June 13, 1931, the Pensacola

Bridge Company—franchised by Escambia and Santa Rosa counties—opens the three-mile $2.5 million concrete toll bay bridge from Pensacola to the Santa Rosa peninsula, the $250,000 wooden Santa Rosa Sound bridge and the $150,000 Casino on Santa Rosa Island. Bridge crusaders Michael A. Touart and O. H. L. (Dad) Wernicke inspire the beach-opening movement, made possible in 1927 by the Florida legislature. The bridge company secures its investment from a lease for two-and-one-half miles on the island to develop the Casino resort. Chamber of Commerce President A. C. Blount, bridge dedication speaker, calls the beach opening "one of the greatest historic events of our city and many historic events have happened here."

The network of roads and bridges lead to eventual routing of the coastal highway (U.S. 98) through Naval Live Oaks Reservation to open beaches at Camp Walton and Panama City, and the paving of U.S. Highway 90 (Old Spanish Trail) from Jacksonville across the Gulf Coast.

Newport Company, naval stores manufacturer using new techniques for extraction of resins and turpentine from stumps, quietly acquires west-side acreage under the guise of developing a chicken farm lest Pensacolians oppose an industrial intrusion on the peace and beauty of the old city. But Newport lifts economic hopes in 1916, employing more than two hundred workers and processing 150 tons of wood a day as Pensacola's first major industrial plant. Yet, with Florida turpentine woods diminishing, Savannah, Georgia, and Jacksonville are far surpassing Pensacola in naval stores trade.

After America enters World War I, fifteen hundred workers build steel merchant marine ships under a more than $15 million federal contract at the new Pensacola Shipyard on Bayou Chico. The Gulf, Florida & Alabama Railroad completes a spur track to the yard, and the Escambia Commissioners install a lift bridge over the bayou. In anticipation of five thousand employment in shipbuilding, and aeronautical station expansion, the federal government spends $750,000 for housing between H and O streets; the war mobilization increases population by ten thousand in two years—totalling thirty-one thousand.

But the economic boom rests on military expenditures; the port's commercial business declines. In the 1920s, Alabamians authorize their legislature to spend $10 million on harbors and seaports, and Mobile aggressively surpasses

Pensacola with new piers, warehouse, and a new terminal railway—all spurring new industrial development. Pensacola fails to modernize wharves, depending heavily on L & N, and can not effectively compete with Mobile, Alabama's only gulf outlet at the base of an extensive river system, and strengthened by favorable rates from the Alabama Railroad Commission.

After World War I, shipbuilding declines, ending in 1926. Mahogany log importer Weis-Patterson (later Weiss-Fricker) locates manufacturing operations on Bayou Chico, and Newport develops a new division, Armstrong-Newport. But International Paper Company—wooed by Pensacolians—chooses instead to build its pulpwood mill at Panama City. Still, Pensacolians are optimistic for marine commerce expansion when the St. Louis-San Francisco (Frisco) Railroad purchases the Muscle Shoals, Birmingham & Pensacola Railroad (originally Gulf, Florida & Alabama) on July 7, 1925, and begins dock renovations to accommodate ocean-going vessels. Frisco's first passenger train arrives to cheering crowds on June 28, 1928, signalling not only the second passenger service but arrival of a national line ending the L & N port monopoly.

In 1920, the *Journal* had warned: "There should be a port commission with authority granted to it by the state made up of men who want to see Pensacola grow. There are a few men of this type in Pensacola. The citizens voted a bond issue several years ago, but no action has been taken by the city government."

Owned by Lois K. Mayes, widow of Frank Mayes, the *Pensacola Journal* is even more visionary when Kentuckian John Holliday Perry, a New York-Palm Beach lawyer-newspaper owner, and Richard Lloyd Jones purchase both the *Journal* and *The Daily News* in 1922, ending Pensacola's last newspaper rivalry that began in 1898. Perry buys out his partner and combines *The Daily News* and *Journal* into the News-Journal Company in 1924. *News-Journal* editorials provide leadership for bridging Escambia Bay to eliminate ferry passage to Santa Rosa County; paving U.S. Highway 90 across West Florida; and developing a scenic route, U.S. Highway 98, along the Gulf Coast to open Panama City and eventually Fort Walton Beach as seaside resorts and ultimately home of new Perry newspapers. Perry's ownership gives West Florida its first major group newspaper operation. Yet, Florida's first press baron considers himself an "improver," envisioning Pensacola as

Charles H. Bliss served as mayor of Pensacola and produced the Bliss Quarterly, *a promotional magazine that preserved many photos and stories about Pensacola at the turn of the century.*
Pensacola Historical Society

Palafox Street at Garden gives a rare view of the First Methodist Church that was replaced by the San Carlos Hotel in 1910. Note the drainage ditches.
T. T. Wentworth, Jr.

a future port and manufacturing center of consequence with the image of a resort metropolis. Perry Newspapers own the *News-Journal* until July 1969, when John H. Perry, Jr., son of the founder, sells the company to Gannett Company, Inc. for $15.5 million and dissolves his family's newspaper operation.

Radio listeners hear City Clerk John E. Frenkel from the third floor of City Hall on the night of February 3, 1926, announcing the city government's new station WCOA (Wonderful City of Advantages). With Frenkel the sole announcer, and featuring local talent and news, the city hopes its venture into radio will weld the community together. But in the early 1930s, with declining revenues, the City Council sells WCOA to businessman John C. Pace for $6,500. Moving studios to the seventh floor of Hotel San Carlos, Pace develops WCOA as the first commercial radio station, eventually acquired by John H. Perry Newspapers. Yet Frenkel, who in retirement builds the Pensacola Interstate Fair into a major Escambia County fall attraction, is revered by Pensacolians for his role as the "Sunny Boy of the Gulf," launching the city's broadcast industry.

Pensacolians chaffing under Prohibition in the 1920s still find liquor flowing at Sanders Beach, Borocoville, the speakeasies, filling stations, and "soda shops." Liquor smugglers and moonshine manufacturers working the dense woods find a prosperous market in the Navy town; and "shinny" merchant Sam Clepper becomes a Pensacola legend by courteously delivering jugs in brown bags or selling five-gallon kegs for ten dollars for cash-and-carry customers venturing near Clepper's Perdido Bay place.

The Isis and Bonita movie theaters entertain with silent film stars Rudolph Valentino, Mary Pickford, and Harold Lloyd. Even though Pensacolians miss the cultural fare of the Opera House, shattered in the 1916 hurricane, they see the salvaged bricks forming two thirds of the exterior walls of the Spanish Baroque Saenger Theatre on Palafox Street. For thirteen months Pensacolians watch contractors C. H. Turner and G. O. Brosnaham, Jr., build the Palafox architectural landmark. The April 2, 1925 grand opening reveals an ornate Moorish interior decor created from materials, paints, and artistry from Europe, and a star's position for the curved, sculptured Opera House balcony rail. Amid banks of flowers and throngs of dignitaries, patrons in 2,250 seats hear laudatory

speeches and the pipes of the $80,000 Robert Morton organ and see Cecille B. DeMille's silent film epic, *The Ten Commandments*.

Continuing the Opera House tradition, hoofers, baggy-pants comedians, operetta singers, and Broadway actors perform on stage; the Saenger screens Hollywood silent films, talkies, Golden Age classics, and big-screen spectaculars until the projectors stop and darkness falls in 1975.

ABC Southeastern Theaters donates the theater to the city. A city-appointed Saenger Management Board rallies support for a $1.6 million restoration project from Saenger patrons, community leaders, corporations, the University of West Florida, and from federal revenue-sharing and preservation grants. On September 26, 1981, Pensacolians reopen the Grande Dame of Palafox—originally costing $500,000—as a community performing arts theater. With a performance of the Duke Ellington Orchestra directed by Mercer Ellington, Florida's showplace is back in lights; it provides an anchor for cultural arts program and the downtown Renaissance of the 1980s.

The three-member City Commission created in 1913 lapses into municipal discord and political and racial bickering in the late 1920s. After an explosive campaign, Pensacolians heavily endorse a city manager-council charter on July 21, 1931. Only the southside—four precincts near the port—backs the status quo, while North and East Hill deliver 60 percent of the seventy-three hundred votes for ten councilmen representing five wards and the appointment of a professional city manager. The council hires George Roark of Beaumont, Texas, who begins a new municipal government era. The council charter continues into the 1990s.

Pensacolians create special tax districts for establishing schools in the 1920s—an incentive for relocating Pensacola High School from embarrassing, inadequate classrooms in the converted tabernacle of revivalist Gypsy Smith into the new $273,000 Pensacola High School on the slope of Palafox Hill. The new PHS, reflecting strict standards of popular Principal John H. Workman from 1920 to 1945, sets the pattern for Escambia School District school construction accelerating after World War II.

With a government payroll—more than one thousand military personnel and civilians working at the air station and the new Corry Field in the 1930s—many Pensacolians voice the attitude that their city is depression-proof. Despite hun-

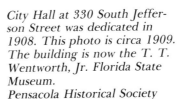

City Hall at 330 South Jefferson Street was dedicated in 1908. This photo is circa 1909. The building is now the T. T. Wentworth, Jr. Florida State Museum.
Pensacola Historical Society

The city of Pensacola bought its first street sprinkler in 1911. Surely the citizens blessed the city father's attempts to keep the dust down.
T. T. Wentworth, Jr.

A cartoon in the Pensacola News-Journal marks the rededication of Old City Hall as the T. T. Wentworth, Jr. Florida State Museum on March 5, 1988. Known as "Mr. History," Wentworth began collecting historical artifacts as a youth during the decade the City Hall was built. Mr. Wentworth was present for the rededication and opening in 1988; he died July 16, 1989, at age 90.
Pensacola News-Journal Files

Kiwanians at a picnic dated September 11, 1919.
Pensacola Historical Society

dreds unemployed from the Crash of 1929, the first Greater Pensacola Open Tournament with a purse of $3,500 at Pensacola Country Club attracts Joey Kirkwood, Ed Dudley, Sammy Snead, and Gene Sarazen; and baseball fans in the wooden grandstand of Legion Field follow the fortunes of the popular Pensacola Fliers in the Class B Southeastern League. The Fliers, led by popular Texan Wally Dashiell, fill Pensacola summers from 1927 until the league is disbanned in 1950, winning league championships in 1928, 1937, 1939, and 1946.

Yet the Great Depression years are hard and slow. With four thousand unemployed in the summer of 1931, Hoovervilles—hobo cities— spring up near the L & N rail tracks at Seventeenth Avenue and south of Cervantes in West Pensacola. By 1933 Pensacola suffers Depression miseries plaguing America. The Pensacola Community Chest, organized in 1925, provides relief funds—$27,000, although it fails its $40,000 goal. The Kiwanis Club supplies free milk for schools. And people chopping wood for the poor find lodging and meals at the Salvation Army. Diminishing voluntary relief in 1932 alarms John H. Sherrill of the unemployment committee: 322 of 672 Escambia County families are destitute, with 2,688 children without sufficient food for four months.

But when Franklin D. Roosevelt becomes president in 1932, New Deal relief funds put almost five thousand Pensacolians back to work. The three banks reopen, youths enter public service at the Fort Barrancas Civilian Conservation Corps Center, and businesses find hope for revitalization through the National Recovery Administration.

Projects of the Federal Emergency Relief Act put relief workers on city-improvement jobs for thirty cents an hour, improving the Baylen Street drainage system, building the Seventeenth Avenue underpass and widening many streets, including Barrancas Avenue from Garden Street to Bayou Chico. Under the Civil Works Administration, almost three thousand workmen share in the $50,000-a-year payroll. Nearly a hundred men build the $300,000 Cervantes Street viaduct. Millions of dollars invigorate the local economy for construction of Bayou Texar Boulevard, O Street (later renamed Pace Boulevard), Lakeview Avenue in East Hill, Innerarity Road, and completion of Barrancas Avenue from Bayou Chico to Bayou Grande. Relief funds provide cultural opportunities—adult education, Pensa-

cola Little Theatre, Federal Art Gallery (which becomes the Pensacola Art Museum in 1940), historical research, and the establishment of the Pensacola Public Library with 4,117 books in 1938. Vestry men of Old Christ Church, inspired by Lelia Abercrombie, provide the 1832 church building for a $1 purchase by the city in 1932 for the WPA library project.

Organized in the Shangtung Room of Hotel San Carlos in 1933, the Pensacola Historical Society is the inspiration of its first president, Henry Clay Armstrong, author of the popular *History of Escambia County, Florida*. The budding society, locating and marking historical landmarks and crusading for their preservation, heightens historical interest by unveiling the first Andrew Jackson memorial in Plaza Ferdinand in 1935, and placing the Alexander McGillivray burial marker at the Panton Leslie site. And T. T. Wentworth, Jr., succeeding Armstrong as president, emerges as the city's legendary crusader for historical recognition and preservation. He promotes the post-World War II revival of the society, which in 1957 honors him as president emeritus.

After President Roosevelt's 1938 visit, Tom A. (Smokestack) Johnson and Michael A. Touart help the Pensacola Housing Authority obtain federal funds for public housing that opens in 1940—Camelia Court (Attucks Court) on West Cervantes for black tenants; Azalea (Aragon Court) for low-income white families; and Moreno Court, off-base military housing east of Corry Field, costing more than $600,000. Pensacola's new Spanish-decor post office building, costing $450,000 in a PWA project, rises at Palafox and Chase streets, symbolic of the Roosevelt New Deal when Postmaster James A. Farley dedicates the landmark structure in January 1940.

In 1937, the *Journal* cheers arrival of "good times," saying the Great Depression is merely history. With the automobile giving Pensacolians mobility—fourteen thousand auto tags issued in 1936, five thousand more than in 1934— Pensacolians find entertainment beyond the Hotel San Carlos dining and dance parties; they frequent Gulf Beach, Paradise Inn on Perdido Bay, the Casino on Santa Rosa Island, the popular Scenic Terrace for teenagers on the bluffs of East Pensacola Heights, and Floridatown across Escambia Bay in Santa Rosa County. With Works Progress Administration and Public Works Administration expanding NAS construction, Pensacola's economy is recovering when war in

This well-known photograph of the Palafox and Garden intersection shows a fountain used for watering horses circa 1910. The Blount Building on the left and the San Carlos Hotel on the right.
Pensacola Historical Society

1909 Picture Palafox and Garden sts showing Frentan

The San Carlos Hotel was constructed in 1910. This view shows the expansion made in the late twenties to the original.
Pensacola Historical Society

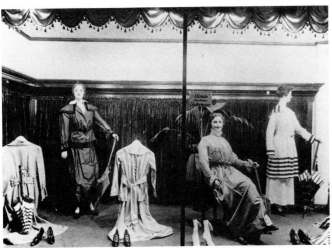

Silverberg's clothing store display window on South Palafox circa 1915.
Pensacola Historical Society

W. B. Harbeson, president of W. B. Harbeson Lumber Company in DeFuniak Springs, was also builder and surveyor of hotels such as the San Carlos Hotel in Pensacola and the Harbeson Hotel in Camp Walton.
Florida State Archives

Europe spurs buildup for naval aviation.

Eager to revive shipbuilding, Pensacolians find the Navy's training priorities prohibit any industrial activity until lifting of the federal ban in 1942. But a year later the Pensacola Shipyard and Engineering Company is in receivership. Reorganized as Smith Shipyards, Inc., in 1944, ship construction never regains its World War I momentum.

Yet John C. Pace, whose family moved to Pensacola in 1906 and by the 1930s had acquired more than one hundred thousand acres of timber land, much of it in Santa Rosa County, provides the impetus for Pensacola industrial development by establishing the Florida Pulp and Paper Company in 1939. James H. Allen, experienced in Georgia's paper-making industry joins Pace as company president and plant manager. The Cantonment mill produces its first paper on August 19, 1941; by 1945, with plans for a million-dollar expansion, Florida Pulp and Paper estimates sales at $6 million from daily production of more than 185 tons daily.

Development of Pensacola's first major industry sets the pattern for the post-World War II economic recruitment. The city purchases the Cantonment acreage, Escambia Commissioners build access roads, and Frisco Railroad provides rail connections to the plant financed by a $1.9 million loan from the Reconstruction Finance Corporation. Pensacola lawyer J. McHenry Jones organizes financial arrangements, based on local investments, a coalition of land holdings—including Henry Hilton-Green's thirty-five thousand acres of timberland—and a state tax exemption. Florida Pulp and Paper repays the city within a few years, and the Pace-Allen company aligns with fast-developing St. Regis Company.

Wartime commerce spurs coal, refined oil, fuel oil, and asphalt shipments through the port—and in 1943 the Civic Roundtable cooperates with Senate President Philip D. Beall and the West Florida legislative delegation to create the municipal Pensacola Port Authority. Beall, a controversial Pensacola lawyer who unsuccessfully challenged the constitutionality of Florida's Prohibition Law in 1919, emerges as a Senate power from 1934 to 1943 and is championed for governor. When the senator who removed the toll from the Thomas D. Johnson Pensacola Bay Bridge dies of a heart attack in December 1943, the *Journal* characterizes Beall as "the hub of politics in the county," a man many thought was next in line for the governorship.

Escambia County's population soars from 74,667 to 106,686 from 1940 to 1945. Most newcomers finding jobs in Navy-related activity locate in suburban areas bordering Pensacola city limits, including three hundred houses in the Navy Point subdivision in 1944. City residents increase from 37,449 to 43,579. The hurried pace of the Pensacola metropolitan area brings ration cards, blackouts, "central war time," victory gardens, and shortages of sugar, meat, gasoline, and tires. The Chamber of Commerce and the War Production Board enlist residents to collect discarded pots and pans, aluminum, tin cans, paper, rags, and rubber for the war effort. Besides salvage parades, Boy Scouts collect scrap metal in neighborhoods for the giant Palafox Street collection pen, and the Navy donates fifty tons of antique cannon, anchors, and metal artifacts. A $3 million War Bond drive yields $8.025 million, and patriotic women serve as hospital and Red Cross volunteers, package "Bundles for Britain," and staff the Pensacola Depot information bureau and USO facilities on Spring, Palafox, and DeVilliers streets.

When World War II ends, Pensacola is a changed city, aware of its substantial Navy economy. And the Pensacola Area Chamber of Commerce launches a three-pronged strategy that remains unchanged in the 1980s: protect naval installations, expand existing industry, attract new industry.

In the post-war 1940s and early 1950s, with Adm. Charles P. Mason as mayor and Oliver J. Semmes as city manager, Pensacola begins a new era, launching ambitious municipal projects that contrast sharply with the financial frugality of the 1930s. Semmes, a native Pensacolian who had been city engineer in the 1930s, negotiates purchase of the natural gas franchise from Gulf Power Company for $1.75 million, and city gas profits finance sanitary sewers and a sewage treatment station, expand water services, and widen and pave streets. Under Semmes' leadership, the City Council reorganizes the police department; builds a new police headquarters, five new fire stations and a new library; and forecasts the bayfront expansion by purchasing additional waterfront property for a port terminal, and building Municipal Auditorium on Palafox Pier. City population doubles in less than fifteen years. Water customers increase from 12,000 to 27,000; gas customers from 8,000 to 34,000. In 1950, city residents number 43,500, with another 69,000 in the county. In 1961, the *Journal* praises the retiring Semmes for inspiring and financing "phenomenal progress" with "little additional taxation."

The spread of suburban growth—Cordova park, East Pensacola Heights, Gulf Breeze on the Santa Rosa peninsula, Pensacola Beach, and the eastern shore of Escambia Bay—marks the coming of Town and Country Plaza with the modern Gayfers' department store north of the city in 1956. The trend toward suburban malls—Cordova and University malls in the 1970s—rapidly erodes the old downtown business district. In the mid-1970s, the city and surviving downtown merchants fear vacant storefronts may have signalled the demise of the city's traditional shopping district. Yet spreading urbanization leads to a county population of 235,000 with 58,000 in the city in the early 1980s.

In the 1950s, the Pensacola Port Authority improves docks, warehouses, and transportation facilities, working to stabilize marine commerce. The L & N and Frisco railroads sell most of their port property to the city. But the devastating November 1, 1958 fire cripples operations. Rebuilt from amongst the wood ashes, the modern Dudley Hunt Marine Terminal processes nitrates, pine products, hardwoods, steel shipments, bulk agricultural products, paper, and oil from new wharves and rail tracks.

Yet, when the city becomes directly involved in port management, the port authority is abolished. In the mid-1970s cargo tonnage soars from 270,000 tons a year in the 1960s to 1.5 million tons in the 1970s, with more than 50 percent of bagged food exports shipped through Pensacola.

During the 1950s, Pensacolians see their dream of industrial expansion unfold, led by Chemstrand, Inc., with a nylon filament plant on a two-thousand-acre site along Escambia River. In 1953, Chemstrand—later Monsanto Textiles Company—is shipping nylon from Pensacola. Monsanto expands with a research and development center, becoming the state's second largest industrial employer with a work force of six thousand.

Two other chemical companies—Escambia Chemical Corporation (1955; Air Products and Chemicals, Inc., 1969) and American Cyanamid Company (1958) build plants along Escambia Bay in Santa Rosa County. And hopes soar for a stronger industrial economy when Westinghouse Corporation builds a $10 million facility to build components for the expanding nuclear power

A grocery store interior on North Davis circa 1929. At left is John Klusscio, and at right is Pete A. Stamatelos.
Pensacola Historical Society

Sherrill Oil serviced vehicles in the station at Garden and Spring in the twenties.
Historic Pensacola Preservation Board

Nightclub interior circa 1942-1945. Note signs "Buy War Bonds" and "No Ladies Allowed in This Place Without Gentlemen Escort."
Pensacola Historical Society

industry at Laura Point on Scenic Highway in 1967.

With Florida building a post-war system of junior colleges, Pensacola High School Principal J. L. McCord launches Pensacola Junior College with a $40,000 budget in the Aiken House on Palafox and Cervantes Street with 128 students on September 8, 1948. Due to racial segregation, Dr. G. T. Wiggins, popular black educator, establishes Washington Junior College in 1949.

With increasing enrollment in 1953, Dr. Henry Ashmore, the first full-time PJC president, moves the college into the former Pensacola High School building. Charting a ten-year expansion program, the popular young administrator increases enrollment to almost four thousand, and the city and the Baars family estate provide the eighty-acre campus near Municipal Airport.

Under Wiggins' pioneering leadership, Washington Junior College meets black students' needs until the segregated college is absorbed into PJC in 1965. Ashmore's successor, T. Felton Harrison, helps bring PJC into the state system and develop plans for Warrington and Milton campuses. With Dr. Horace E. (Ed) Hartsell as president in 1980, PJC is one of Florida's largest community colleges, providing academic, technical, vocational, and adult education for more than twenty thousand students.

Yet many Pensacolians envision PJC expansion into a four-year school when the 1955 Florida legislature authorizes the state Board of Control to establish a university in Escambia County. Governor Farris Bryant, John C. Pace of the Board of Control, and Escambia legislators strongly endorse a separate institution, and Pensacolians fashion a compromise. After the 1963 legislature appropriates $2.1 million for a regional senior university in the Pensacola area, Escambia Commissioners approve a bond issue to purchase the thousand-acre wooded Riverview campus near the Escambia River for The University of West Florida. A native Pensacolian, former Circuit Court Judge Harold Bryan Crosby, who had taught in the University of Florida Law School, becomes charter president, overseeing the rise of university buildings from 1965 until he welcomes more than fifteen hundred students for the first classes on September 25, 1967. UWF names its library—architectural focus of the campus—for John C. Pace, whose work on the Board of Control inspired establishment of Florida's first university west of Tallahassee.

Under Crosby, UWF mounts an extensive outreach program, fashioning a process of junior college cooperative programs that becomes a model for the state. UWF leads in serving the older "non-traditional" students of the post-Vietnam era and supports the increasing role of women and minorities in the work place.

In 1974, Dr. James A. Robinson, former president of MacAlester College in Minnesota, succeeds Crosby as president. Robinson encourages research, a more traditional curriculum, and works for its lower division expansion with freshmen and sophomores in 1983. After the UWF Panama City campus joins with Florida State University, Robinson focuses on developing a branch facility at Fort Walton Beach.

Both Crosby and Robinson become regent faculty scholars when Dr. Morris L. Marx becomes UWF's third president on February 15, 1988. With enrollment more than seven thousand in the late 1980s, Marx shares with Pensacolians the goal of higher education becoming an active partner with the community and West Florida region for economic and cultural enrichment for the 1990s and twenty-first century.

Escambia Commissioners build the first county hospital, Escambia General (later renamed University Hospital) in 1948, and with the opening of Baptist Hospital in 1951 and creation of the Medical Center Clinic, Pensacola enters an era of expanded medical facilities north of the city. Besides the modern Sacred Heart Hospital on Ninth Avenue (1965), the Medical Center Clinic on North Palafox Street joins Hospital Corporation of America to build the West Florida Regional Medical Center in the mid-1970s. In the 1980s, Pensacola's comprehensive medical facilities serve the West Florida/South Alabama region with a growing reputation for health care rivaling Birmingham, Mobile, New Orleans, and Gainesville.

Nagging the multi-ethnic city since early in the twentieth century, racial separation slowly diminishes with the 1960s civil rights movement and court litigation eventually integrating all-white Oliver J. Semmes Elementary School. Dr. and Mrs. Charles A. Augustus break the Escambia County racial barrier for their daughter Karen, a first grader, in the first class-action integration suit filed in Florida.

The News Journal, which had advocated school desegregation before the 1954 Supreme Court ruling, encourages peaceful acceptance of all Americans, and the U.S. Navy demands equi-

T. T. WENTWORTH, JR.
MUSEUM

Opening of the Pensacola Bay Bridge
celebration, 1931.
T. T. Wentworth, Jr.

Pensacola Bay Bridge, 1930s.
Pensacola Historical Society

Casino, Pensacola Beach 1930s.
Pensacola Historical Society

table treatment for all races. Demonstrators protest segregated lunch counters at the downtown J. J. Newberry store, and early desegregation efforts at Escambia and Woodham high schools ignite minor racial confrontations. But in the mid-1970s blacks attain their rightful status in the community and share the governmental leadership. Hollis Williams breaks the racial barrier as the first black on the City Council, and Willie Junior—first black elected to the Escambia County Commission—serves as commission chairman in the 1980s. Cecil Hunter, black school administrator, serves as mayor pro tem in the 1980s.

Pensacola produces an American black military hero, Air Force pilot Daniel (Chappie) James Jr., 1937 graduate of segregated Washington High School and the first of his race to wear the four stars of full general in the American military. Born on February 11, 1920, Chappie James learns his appreciation for education under the stern guidance of his mother, Lillie James, who began a private black school in 1900 so her children and other neighborhood blacks could attain at least an eighth-grade education. Graduating from Tuskegee Institute in 1942, James hones his desire to fly by instructing Army Air Corps cadets at Tuskegee, earning his commission as a second lieutenant in 1943. Battling racial discrimination, the burly Pensacolian rises in rank as a combat pilot in Korea and Vietnam. In the early 1970s, James achieves national attention for patriotic speeches while serving as deputy assistant secretary of defense (for public affairs) and commanding general of all United States and Canadian strategic aerospace defense forces. A believer in the American dream, General James said he won his four stars "because I'm damned good." Always a champion for equality, and with faith in American justice, James tells fellow blacks to share his belief in the "power of excellence." The popular good-will ambassador receives numerous national honors before his retirement—and sudden death—in 1978.

Conservative politics are a tradition with many Pensacolians, even though registered Democrats dominate local elections after the rise of the party in the aftermath of Reconstruction. Yet, from the 1960s to the 1980s, West Floridians—supporting Barry Goldwater, Richard Nixon, Gerald Ford, Ronald Reagan, and George Bush for president—find the new-wave GOP more acceptable to their basic conservatism. Yet, despite growing interest in a two-party system, the old

Democratic party system dominates Escambia County politics from the 1900s through the 1980s. And the Democrats produce their share of state leaders, including George Stone of Walnut Hill, chosen Speaker of the Florida House of Representatives before his tragic death in a 1967 automobile accident; Reubin O'Donovan Askew, serving in both the Florida House and Senate before becoming the first Florida governor to serve two consecutive terms (1971-1979); and Wyon Dale (W. D.) Childers, sharing with Philip Beall the stature of Senate president.

Reubin Askew, born in Oklahoma in 1928, is nine when his mother moves the family back to her native Pensacola in 1937. A graduate of Pensacola High School and Florida State University, Askew obtains his law degree from the University of Florida. He serves as Escambia County solicitor before launching a distinguished career as Florida legislator and one of Florida's most popular governors—frequently described as having presidential potential. He serves as U.S. Trade Ambassador in President Jimmy Carter's administration, and in 1984 is among Democratic candidates for party presidential nomination before abandoning the campaign for private law practice in Miami and Orlando. Even though Askew's moderate position often troubled Escambians, his personal popularity at home matches his Florida political stature as one of modern Florida's most respected politicians.

Historical preservation of the 1960s, cleanup of polluted Escambia Bay, and development of parks—specifically Gulf Islands National Seashore—sets the stage for Pensacola's downtown Renaissance in the 1970s and 1980s. And a far-reaching American Revolution Bicentennial program, Action '76, crystallizes the revitalization projects with a citizens' goals-setting movement.

First suggested in *News-Journal* editorials in the early 1960s, the national seashore campaign triggers an eight-year struggle between environmentalists, wanting the unspoiled beaches of Santa Rosa Island for a national park, and real estate developers, the Pensacola Area Chamber of Commerce, and radio station WCOA preferring local control and beach development.

Opponents galvanize against the *News-Journal,* with support from WCOA and Chamber leaders; but finally a straw-ballot on transferring county-held Santa Rosa beaches to the national seashore shows overwhelming support for the National Park Service. And political opposition fades.

Led in Congress by Crestview's Bob Sikes, who

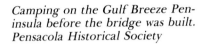

Pensacola manufacturer Kras-
noski made special beach
sandals in the 1930s.
Pensacola Historical Society

Camping on the Gulf Breeze Peninsula before the bridge was built.
Pensacola Historical Society

The Lysistrata was used as a ferry to
Gulf Breeze in 1946 when the bridge
was struck and temporarily out of use.
Pensacola Historical Society

Dr. J. C. Heinberg, first mayor of
Gulf Breeze, being sworn in at the
first Gulf Breeze City Hall (the old
Duncan house) in 1961. He is greeted
by Congressman Bob Sikes (left).
Pensacola Historical Society

calls passage of the legislation his "proudest moment in Congress," the Seashore preserving twenty-one miles of Santa Rosa and Perdido Key beaches and the Pensacola harbor forts becomes an active, developing national recreational park after President Richard Nixon signs the Seashore Act in January 8, 1971. In less than ten years, Forts Pickens and Barrancas, Spanish Battery San Antonio, and the Barrancas Redoubt are restored as national monuments. In the 1980s, seashore beaches in Florida and Mississippi, and Pensacola harbor forts make Gulf Islands one of the most visited seacoast parks in the national system.

The Seville preservation movement—set in motion by plans developed by the City Council's Advisory Committee on Historical Development—leads to the establishment of the Pensacola Historical District and the creation of the Pensacola Historical Restoration and Preservation Commission (later renamed the Historic Pensacola Preservation Board) by the Florida legislature in 1967. The preservation agency acquires historical properties and develops museums in the twenty-seven-block Seville District. With guidance from a city architectural review board, property owners begin restoring Creole cottages and Old City landmark buildings reflective of the nineteenth century. Seville becomes Pensacola's popular heritage area, scene for festivals—inspired by the Pensacola Heritage Foundation's "An Evening in Old Seville Square" on August 17, 1967, attracting more than twenty thousand persons for the first memorable celebration for the preservation of Old Pensacola.

Slowly, historical restoration spreads to other pockets of downtown Pensacola—first to North Hill, where residents organize the North Hill Preservation Association and ask the City Council to establish the second preservation district; then to Palafox Street for the revitalized historic business district known as Palafox Place.

Bicentennial excitement motivates Pensacola visionaries in the 1970s, and citizens' goals include building scenic Bayfront Parkway and reclamation of the Pensacola bayfront, completion of Interstate 10 across West Florida and Interstate 110 into downtown Pensacola, restoration of the Saenger Theatre, Pensacola Civic Center, and downtown redevelopment.

In the 1980s, Pensacola and Escambia County invest $31 million in public improvements, including the $21 million Pensacola Civic Center, and a new $8 million City Hall. The $14 million Pensacola Hilton Hotel rises as a fifteen-story tower attached to the restored old L & N passenger station adjacent to the ten-thousand-seat Pensacola Civic Center. And the city begins the bayfront revitalization with private-business partnerships for Port Royal condominiums and marina, and six-story Harbourview Office Building at Baylen Street Slip, and Pitt Slip Marina, and Harbour Place commercial development south of Bayfront Parkway.

Old City Hall, renovated with a $1.2 million state grant from the Florida legislature, houses the T. T. Wentworth, Jr., Florida State Museum, flagship of the Pensacola Historical Village spreading across the Seville district between Plaza Ferdinand and Seville Square. Continuing preservation projects reflect the vision and goals of many historians and activists, among them Quadricentennial promoter/lawyer John McHenry Jones, educator Occie Clubbs, community visionary Mayhew (Pat) Dodson and Pensacola Heritage Foundation leader Mary Turner Rule Reed in the 1960s and 1970s and historians/authors Woodward B. (Woody) Skinner and John Appleyard.

Many community activists share Pensacola's New Age leadership in the post-World War II business and community Renaissance, among them popular mayors Charles P. Mason, Reinhardt Holm, Warren Briggs and Vince Whibbs, city councilmen Howard Rein and Michael Bass, contractor/builders William J. (Pete) Noonan Sr., Raymond Dyson and Charles and William Soule, insurance executive David Tobin Johnson, Warrington banker/businessman Charles P. (Chuck) Woodbury, bankers G. Wright Reese and F. M. (Son) Turner, businessman/banker James H. Baroco, Coca Cola bottler/downtown developer Crawford Rainwater, Mutual Federal President Elbert W. Hopkins, state legislators J. B. Hopkins, James Reeves, Gordon Wells and Virginia Bass, Gayfers store manager Charles Schuster, Chamber of Commerce leaders M. J. Menge and Carl C. Mertins, industrialist Marvin Kaiman, merchants Nathan Kahn and Albert Klein, Westinghouse pioneer William H. Griffith, port advocate E. P. (Ted) Nickinson, Jr., Baptist Hospital pioneer Pat Groner, Pensacola Hilton Hotel founder Robert Windham, Children's Hospital pioneer Dr. Reed Bell, fishing fleet operator Joe Patti and popular Seville Quarter creator Robert (Bob) Snow.

Now a *second* New Pensacola skyline rises from Old Pensacola architecture on centuries-old streets, blending its long Gulf Coast heritage with ambitions for *new* economic vitality as a national tourist-destination city. Saving and preserving its seacoast gifts of nature and historical landmarks, Pensacola looks beyond its substantial U.S. Navy economy.

Pensacola during the post-World War II rehabilitative years—1950s to the 1980s—sharply contrasts with the emerging New South city on the dawn of the twentieth century. Yet, visionaries in the centuries-old seaport on the threshold of the last decade of the twentieth century share with city ancestors a dream awaiting fulfillment.

Newport Turpentine and Resin Company came to Pensacola in 1916. Pensacola's first production industry, it processed resin and turpentine from pine stumps. Newport was instrumental in bringing Armstrong Cork Company here to process the "spentwood" into fiber insulation board and ceiling tile. The Newport Company has been successively sold to Tenneco and then to Reichold in 1973.
Pensacola Historical Society

Pensacola Shipbuilding Company operated during the World War I era. Here the S. S. Rockport is readied for launching in September 1919.
Pensacola Historical Society

Goulding Fertilizer Company was established by H. M. and W. J. Goulding of Dublin, Ireland, circa 1897-98.
Pensacola Historical Society

Taylor Brick and Tile Company employees in front of the Pensacola brick kiln used to fire bricks manufactured in the thirties and forties. From left to right are Marion Enfinger, H. P. Brewer, Henry Enfinger, Albert Caro, Claude Ward, Floyd Ellard Smith, Woodrow Allen, George Matthes, Edmond Portorhs, Burl Smith, Essie Wallace, (Buddie) Phillip O'Neal, Preacher Williams, Johnnie Lewis, Robert Watson, J. B. Matthes, Therdo (Theodore) Byrd, Willie Bryant, John Brown, Aaron Bailey, Essie Matthes, Oscar Williams, and Will Taylor.
Pensacola Historical Society

The schooner Silas Sterns of Pensacola was launched December 23, 1897, at Milton, Florida.
Pensacola Historical Society

Gulf Breeze marine railroad workers posed for this picture circa 1905. In the back row only George Meker (15), at the far left, is identified. In the second row those identified are Armour Prout (4), second from the left; James Balkum (5), third from the left; David Balkum (6), fourth from the left; Harry Harrison (12), sixth from the left; and Monroe Balkum (8), eighth from the left. Identified in the third row are Frank Duncan (13), at the far left; Jonas Anderson (14), second from the left; Ralph Duncan (17), sixth from the left; Charlie White (16), seventh from the left; John Walch (19), tenth from the left; and John Balkum (7), far right. In the front row, Wallie Jordan (2) and Robert Duncan (18) are identified.
Pensacola Historical Society

Spearman Brewing Company began production in 1935. It ceased to bottle beer in Pensacola in the early 1960s.
Pensacola Historical Society

Breen family members circa 1930s.
Florida State University photo

Spearman Straight Eight Beer cone top can. Cone top cans were used by breweries from the 1930s to the 1950s.
Pensacola Historical Society

In 1932 the Pensacola Coach Corporation began service with seven coaches. The fare was five cents.
Pensacola Historical Society

Manager Wally Dashiell's Pensacola Fliers baseball team at Legion Field in the 1930s.
Pensacola Historical Society

Boyd's Tourist Cottage, January 1941.
Library of Congress, Marion P. Wolcott photo,
Florida State University

Campers enjoy Pensacola in 1945.
Pensacola Historical Society

WCOA ("Wonderful City of Advantages"), the first radio station in Pensacola, was established in 1926. The radio towers were behind City Hall, the city having the first radio license. In 1954 WEAR-TV went on the air to pioneer television in Pensacola.
Pensacola Historical Society

Pensacola Promoters in the 1920s.
Pensacola Historical Society

The Four Stompers who frequently played on WCOA. Left to right are Jack Freeman, piano; Al Moore, trombone; Gene Villar, trumpet; Al Murphy, drums.
Pensacola Historical Society

Eddie Collins' Rainbow Orchestra. Left to right are Johnnie Campodonico, alto saxophone; Sybil McNair, piano;

Frank Howland, banjo; Gene Villar, drums; and Eddie Collins, saxophone.
Pensacola Historical Society

Fairfield Orchestra, 1916. Left to right are Henry Phillips, drums; Ben H. Franklin, bass; Florida Fairchild, piano; Fred L. Fairchild, violin; Mrs. Ben Fairchild, trumpet; and Albert Sheerer, trombone.
Pensacola Historical Society

"Here Comes the Law." It appears law enforcement officials have confiscated a still.
Pensacola Historical Society

Crowd outside the Isis Theatre in the 1920-1930 era.
Pensacola Historical Society

Group of city and county officers. Seated left to right are: unidentified, Adrian Langford, Harvey Bayliss, John E. Frenkel, Ernest Harper, and John B. Jones. Standing in the first row are L. L. Burpers, Len LeBarrow, Tom Finch, Chief William O'Connell, Chief W. R. Bicker, Tom Johnson, Wescott Williams, and Frank Jarrett. Back row are Fred Schad, Jus Largue, Chubby Wells, and the last three people are unidentified.
Historic Pensacola Preservation Board

Ada Wilson, a Pensacola Artist, sold many of her antiques to entertainer Liberace.
Historic Pensacola Preservation Board

Moreno Courts circa 1940.
Pensacola Historical Society

St. Michael's Cemetery dedication of the Dorothy Walton marker February 21, 1929. Children left to right are June Helie, Clarence Quina, Huntley

Elebash, and Phyllis Douglas.
Pensacola Historical Society

The new Pensacola Public Library on Gregory Street opened in 1957. It originated in the Old Christ Church in 1938.
Pensacola Historical Society

A popular gathering spot from the 1930s to the 1960s was the Pensacola Dairy Company. This is a 1950s photo.
Delores Pittman photo

The Old Fire House Restaurant, a former fire station, was also a popular gathering spot in the fifties and sixties. The building has been modified and became the home of McGuire's Irish Pub in the eighties.
T. T. Wentworth, Jr.

Tristan de Luna 1952, J. McHenry Jones, crowns his Queen, Nikki Hayward (Wiltshire), as part of the Fiesta of Five Flags celebration. The Fiesta celebration began in 1950 and continues today as a celebration of Pensacola heritage. Photos of most of the Lunas and queens are on display at New World Landing, a popular restaurant in a restored warehouse on South Palafox.
Pensacola Historical Society

Air Products and Chemicals, Inc., was founded in 1969. It had formerly been Escambia Chemical originally organized along Escambia Bay in 1955.
Pensacola Historical Society

Monsanto nylon and filament yarn plant was founded in 1962; formed from the Chemstrand Company that was founded in 1951.
Pensacola Historical Society

Mayor Erwin Greenhut, grandson of former Mayor Adolph Greenhut, greets gubernatorial candidate Claude Kirk on the steps of City Hall during the 1966 campaign. *Pensacola News-Journal*

The Aiken residence at Palafox and Cervantes streets was the first home of Pensacola Junior College. *Pensacola Historical Society*

Pensacola Junior College campus, 1977. *Pensacola Historical Society*

University of West Florida campus, 1970s.
Pensacola Historical Society

Pensacola publisher and staff prepare their
newspaper in the 1930s.
Pensacola Historical Society

Dr. James Allen, distinguished Pensa-
cola physician.
Pensacola Historical Society

Daniel (Chappie) James, America's first four-star black general. His mother, Lillie James started a private school in 1900 so that her children and other neighborhood blacks might receive proper education. The regional state building on Government Street is named for General James. Pensacola Historical Society

Escambia County State Senator Wyon Dale Childers was known as the "Banty Rooster" during his early senate years as successor to Reubin Askew. The News-Journal cartoon depicts Childers the year he was chosen Senate president (1981). Pensacola News-Journal

Congressman Bob Sikes, Ronald Lee, National Park Service director, and Norman Simons, museum curator, during the survey for the proposed Gulf Islands National Seashore, circa 1965. Pensacola News-Journal Files

Reubin Askew, an attorney from Pensacola, served twelve years in the state legislature and was governor of Florida from 1970 to 1978.
Pensacola News-Journal *Files*

A fact-finding group prepares a report on the proposed Gulf Islands National Seashore, in the early 1960s. Left to right are unidentified; Harry Blanchard; Congressman Bob Sikes; Ellis Bullock; Reinhardt Holm; Allen Rick; Mayor B. Irving Greenhut; Earle Bowden, News-Journal *editor;* unidentified; unidentified; Ronald Lee, Park Service director; Norman Simons, museum curator; Mary Turner Rule, historic preservation leader, who began An Evening in Old Seville Square; Woody Skinner, Pensacola High School history teacher and author; and Capt. A. C. (Cordy) Weart.
Pensacola News-Journal *Files*

The Gulf Islands National Seashore Visitors Center and Headquarters building within the old Naval Oaks Reservation on Highway 98 was dedicated in May 1988.
Gulf Islands National Seashore *photo*

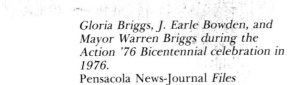

Historic Pensacola Preservation Board members in 1968 were, left to right, H. W. Olcott, Henry Dartigalongue, Earle Bowden, Earle Newton (Director), Ellis Bullock, Jr., and Chairman Pat Dodson.
Historic Pensacola Preservation Board

Gloria Briggs, J. Earle Bowden, and Mayor Warren Briggs during the Action '76 Bicentennial celebration in 1976.
Pensacola News-Journal *Files*

British Sixtieth re-enactment regiment marches past Fort George Park during Bicentennial Galvez Celebration in 1981.
Pensacola News-Journal *Files*

This 1980s aerial shows Interstate 110 spur, the new Pensacola Civic Center, and the L & N passenger station, and new Pensacola Hilton Hotel.
Pensacola Historical Society

"Gone Fishing."
Pensacola Historical Society

Jefferson Street extension runs through a three-block area where the old Pensacola News-Journal had been located. The paper had campaigned editorially for the extension. In 1982 a further extension carried Jefferson from Garden to Chase, giving easier access to I-110 and relieving downtown congestion.
Pensacola News-Journal Files

A variety of sailing and motorized vessels can be seen at the Port of Pensacola circa 1989, though nothing to equal that of the "boom" era when timber was king.
Al Alderman, ASA Photo/Graphics

The new Hilton Hotel rises behind the restored L & N Railroad passenger station that houses the restaurants and offices of the popular hotel, circa 1989.
Al Alderman, ASA Photo/Graphics

The Pensacola Museum of Art is located in the old City Jail on Jefferson Street, circa 1989.
Al Alderman, ASA Photo/Graphics

The Lighthouse located on the Naval Air Station was constructed in 1859 and is now a U.S. Coast Guard Station, within boundaries of Gulf Islands National Seashore, circa 1989.
Al Alderman, ASA Photo/Graphics

Dolphins are frequently seen offshore leaping and following Gulf boats and skiers, circa 1989.
Al Alderman, ASA Photo/Graphics

The restored Saenger Theatre serves as a cultural center along the restored streetscape of Palafox Place, circa 1989.
Al Alderman, ASA Photo/Graphics

Tourists and Pensacolians alike enjoy the entertainers during a patriotic celebration at the popular Seville Quarter and Rosie O'Grady Good Time Emporium on Government Street which connects the restored downtown area to the Seville Square historical district, circa 1989.
Al Alderman, ASA Photo/Graphics

Mardi Gras revelers throw tokens at a parade. Mardi Gras had been celebrated in Pensacola regularly from 1900 to 1930 when it died out. Revived in 1977, it is one of several such celebrations along the Gulf Coast, circa 1989.
Al Alderman, ASA Photo/Graphics

Exterior of Rosie O'Grady's Seville Quarter Entertainment Complex, circa 1989.
Al Alderman, ASA Photo/Graphics

William Dudley Chipley monument in Plaza Ferdinand.
Hemmer and Yates Advertising Agency

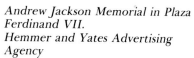

Andrew Jackson Memorial in Plaza Ferdinand VII.
Hemmer and Yates Advertising Agency

Fort Pickens.
Hemmer and Yates Advertising Agency

196

Pensacola proudly flies five flags.
*Hemmer and Yates Advertising
Agency*

Many North Hill residences have been
restored and used either as homes or
businesses in the North Hill Preservation District.
*Hemmer and Yates Advertising
Agency*

Port Royal bayfront condominiums in
the Baylen Street Slip redevelopment
area in the 1980s.
*Hemmer and Yates Advertising
Agency*

197

The Edward Ball Nature Trail at the
University of West Florida offers time
for quiet reflection.
Hemmer and Yates Advertising
Agency

Navy plane.
Hemmer and Yates Advertising
Agency

Seville Square Gazebo is the scene of
many celebrations such as the Greater
Gulf Coast Art Festival usually held in
November.
Hemmer and Yates Advertising
Agency

Overlook at Scenic Bluffs Park on Scenic Highway in the 1980s.
Hemmer and Yates Advertising Agency

Restored buildings on South Palafox in the 1980s.
Hemmer and Yates Advertising Agency

Detail of downtown buildings on South Palafox in the 1980s.
Hemmer and Yates Advertising Agency

A Pensacola sunset.
Hemmer and Yates Advertising
Agency

The Crystal Ice Company building is
one of those unusual structures in
Pensacola that have been placed on
the National Register.
Constance H. Marse

Bibliography
Selected Books

Armstrong, Henry Clay. *History of Escambia County, Florida.* St. Augustine, Florida: The Record Company, 1930.

Bearss, Edwin C. *Gulf Islands: Fort Pickens 1821-1895.* Gulf Islands National Seashore Historic Structure Report (historical data section). Washington, D.C.: National Park Service, 1983.

Bowden, Jesse Earle. *Always the Rivers Flow: Deliberately a Memoir.* Pensacola: University of West Florida Foundation, 1979.

_____, and Alan R. Rick. *Florida in the Civil War: 1860 through Reconstruction.* Pensacola: The Civil War Round Table of Pensacola, 1961.

Caughey, John Walton. *Bernardo de Galvez in Louisiana, 1776-1783.* Gretna, Louisiana: Pelican Publishing Company, 1972.

_____, editor. *McGillivray of the Creeks.* Norman, Oklahoma: University of Oklahoma Press, 1938.

Campbell, Richard L. *Historical Sketches of Colonial Florida.* A facsimile reproduction of 1892 edition. Gainesville, Florida: University Press of Florida, 1975.

Coleman, James C. and Irene S. Coleman. *Guardians on the Gulf: Pensacola Fortifications, 1698-1980.* Pensacola: Pensacola Historical Society, 1982.

Coker, William S. and Thomas D. Watson. *Indian Traders of the Southeastern Spanish Borderlands: Panton, Leslie & Company and John Forbes & Company, 1783-1847.* Gainesville: University Presses of Florida; University of West Florida Press, 1986.

Coker, William S. and G. Douglas Inglis. *The Spanish Censuses of Pensacola, 1784-1820: A Genealogical Guide to Spanish Pensacola.* Pensacola: Perdido Bay Press, 1980.

Currin, Beverly Madison. *From One Generation to Another.* Pensacola: Privately printed, 1977.

Davis, William Watson. *The Civil War and Reconstruction in Florida.* A facsimile reproduction of the 1913 edition. Gainesville: University of Florida Press, 1964.

Dibble, Ernest F. *Antebellum Pensacola and the Military Presence.* Pensacola: Pensacola Series Commemorating the American Revolution Bicentennial, 1974.

Doherty, Herbert J., Jr. *Richard Keith Call: Southern Unionist.* Gainesville: University of Florida Press, 1961.

Dovell, J. E. *Florida: Historic, Dramatic Contemporary.* New York: Lewis Publishing Company, Inc., 1952.

Durkin, Joseph T., S. J. *Stephen R. Mallory, Confederate Navy Chief.* Chapel Hill: University of North Carolina Press, 1954.

Ellsworth, Lucius and Linda Ellsworth. *Pensacola: The Deep Water City.* Tulsa, Oklahoma: Continental Heritage Press, 1982.

Gannon, Michael V. *The Cross in the Sand.* Gainesville: University of Florida Press, 1967.

Holmes, Jack D. L. *Honor and Fidelity.* Birmingham, Alabama. Privated printed, 1965.

James, Marquis. *The Life of Andrew Jackson.* New York: Bobbs-Merrill Company, 1938.

McClellan, Don. *Fifty Years in Pensacola.* n.p. 1944.

McGovern, James R., editor. *Andrew Jackson and Pensacola.* Pensacola: Pensacola Series Commemorating the American Revolution Bicentennial, 1974.

_____, editor. *Colonial Pensacola.* Pensacola: Pensacola Series Commemorating the American Revolution Bicentennial, 1974.

_____, *The Emergence of a City in the Modern South: Pensacola 1900-1945.* Pensacola: University of West Florida Foundation, 1976.

Parks, Virginia. *Pensacola: Spaniards to Space-Age.* Pensacola: Pensacola Historical Society, 1986.

_____, editor. *Iron Horse in the Pinelands: Building West Florida's Railroad: 1881-1883,* Pensacola: Pensacola Historical Society, 1982.

_____, editor. *Siege! Spain and Britain: Battle of Pensacola March 9-May 8, 1781.* Pensacola: Pensacola Historical Society, 1981.

Pearce, George E. *The U.S. Navy in Pensacola: From Sailing Ships to Naval Aviation (1825-1930).* Pensacola: University Press of Florida, 1980.

Pfeiffer, Philip A. *Pensacola's Currency Issuing Banks and Their Bank Notes. 1883-1935.* Pensacola: Pfeiffer Printing Company, 1975.

Priestley, Herbert Ingram, editor. *The Luna Papers. Documents Relating to the Expedition of Don Tristan de Luna y Ayellano for Conquest of La Florida in 1559-1561.* Freeport, New York: Books of Libraries Press, 1971.

Proctor, Samuel, editor. *Eighteenth Century Florida and Its Borderlands.* Gainesville: University Presses of Florida, 1975.

Remini, Robert V. *Andrew Jackson and the Course of American Empire, 1767-1821.* New York: Harper & Row, 1977.

Rerick, Rowland H. *Memoirs of Florida.* Atlanta: The Southern Historical Association, 1902.

Shofner, Jerrill H. *Nor Is It Over Yet: Florida in the Era of Reconstruction 1863-1877.* Gainesville: University Press of Florida, 1974.

Simons, G. Norman and James R. McGovern. *Pensacola in Pictures and Prints.* Pensacola: Pensacola Series Commemorating the American Revolution Bicentennial, 1974.

Skinner, Woodward B. (Woody). *The Apache Rock Crumbles: The Captivity of Geronimo's People.* Pensacola: Skinner Publications, 1987.

_____, *Geronimo at Fort Pickens.* Pensacola: Frank R. Parkhurst & Son Publishing, 1981.

Starr, J. Barton *Tories, Dons & Rebels: The American Revolution in British West Florida.* Gainesville: University Press of Florida, 1976.

Walker, Jonathan. *Trial and Imprisonment of Jonathan Walker at Pensacola, Florida.* Facsimile reproduction of the 1845 edition. Gainesville: University of Florida Presses, 1974.

Williams, John Lee. *A View of West Florida.* A facsimile reproduction of the 1827 edition. Gainesville: Univeristy Presses of Florida, 1976.

Woodward, Ralph Lee, Jr. *Tribute to Don Bernardo de Galvez.* New Orleans: Historic New Orleans Collection, 1979.

Wright, J. Leitch, Jr. *Florida in the American Revolution.* Gainesville: University Presses of Florida, 1975.

Selected Articles

Bowden, Jesse Earle. "The Civil War 100 Years Ago This Week." Sunday Civil War Centennial Series. *Pensacola News Journal.* 1960-65.

_____. "Editors and Other Hell Raisers of West Florida Journalism." *Threads of Tradition and Culture Along the Gulf Coast.* Ronald V. Evans, editor. Volume X, Proceedings of the Gulf Coast History and Humanities Conference (1986): 1-33.

Bears, Edwin C. "Civil War Operations In and Around Pensacola." Parts 1-3. *Florida Historical Quarterly* 36, Nos. 2-4, 1957-58.

Jensen, Leslie D. "Photographer of the Confederacy: J. D. Edwards." *Shadows of the Storm, Volume I of The Image of War: 1861-1865.* The National Historical Society. Garden City, New York: Doubleday & Company (1981): 344-363.

Skinner, Woodward B. "Pensacola's Exiled Government." *Florida Historical Quarterly* 39, no. 3 (January 1961): 270-273.

Ricks, Alan and Norman Simons. "Pensacola in the Civil War." *Pensacola Historical Society Quarterly* IX, No. 2, Spring 1978.

Rosenbleeth, Arnold. Research papers for "A Decade of Decision, 1860-1870." manuscript in progress on Civil War Pensacola, 1988.

Yonge, Phillip Keyes. "The Lumber Industry of West Florida." *Florida Edition, Makers of America.* Atlanta: A. B. Caldwell (1909): 30-78.

Index

About the Authors

Jesse Earle Bowden

Editor and Vice President of the *Pensacola News Journal,* Jesse Earle Bowden is a prize-winning Pensacola editorialist, political cartoonist, book author, and pioneer of Pensacola's historical preservation movement. Bowden helped pioneer the Historic Pensacola Preservation board of Trustees and Gulf Islands National Seashore. Author of the 1979 West Florida memoir, *Always the River Flows,* Bowden's writings and drawings appear in numerous other books and collections. Bowden teaches journalistic writing courses at the University of West Florida as an associate faculty member.

Gordon Norman Simons

Gordon Norman Simons served the Pensacola Historical Society and the Historic Pensacola Preservation Board of Trustees as a curator, pictorial archivist, and archaeologist. As curator-director of the Pensacola Historical Museum he helped establish the T. T. Wentworth Jr. Florida State Museum. Author of numerous papers and articles on Pensacola history, Simons co-authored *Pensacola in Pictures and Prints.* He was selected for the Society's highest honor, the Heritage Award, in 1984. His years-long work of collecting and preserving rare Pensacola historical photographs are reflected on these pages.

Sandra L. Johnson

Sandra L. Johnson, curator of Pensacola Historical Museum since 1988, joined the staff in 1976. She serves as co-editor and contributor to *Pensacola History Illustrated* and has participated in other Pensacola Historical Society publications, including co-author of *Pensacola: The Old and the New, A Guide to Pensacola and Surrounding Areas.*

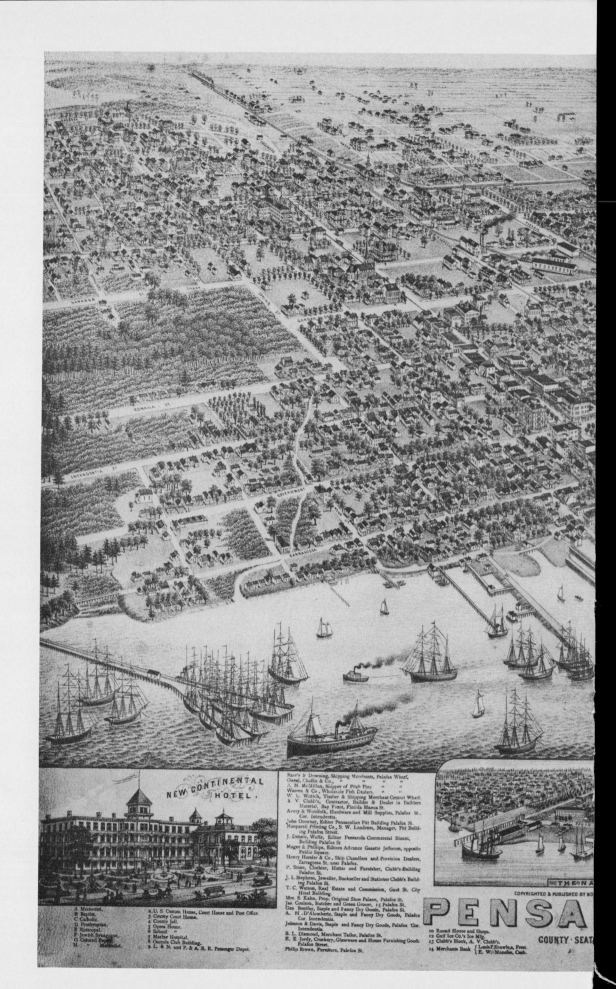